POWERFUL BUSINESS RULES, EXTRAORDINARY RESULTS

How to start, run, manage and future proof a successful business. This book will save you time and money

John Wright
Ligia Turincio

CONTENTS

Title Page
Why YOU Should Read This Book   1
1. How the business world has changed   3
2. Businesses are simple   6
3. How and why businesses start   11
4. Meetings   16
5. What do consumers want?   19
6. let's talk about your offer   35
7. Over delivery, marketing gold - How to make your customers love you   45
8. Marketing trends that you should know about   51
9. Getting new business   65
10. Developing export markets   72
11. Financing your business   85
12. Some final thoughts from those that have already done it   90

WHY YOU SHOULD READ THIS BOOK

Most really useful business ideas are simple and stunningly effective, so simple, that we, as readers, sometimes wonder why we didn't think of them ourselves. The world of business has changed fundamentally bringing huge opportunities for small businesses to get into the game cheaper and faster and for big corporations to engage with their customers in new and productive ways. Smart businesses are embracing the opportunities, many are playing catch up, complying because they have to rather than enjoying the process, and others will not adapt fast enough or radically enough and will disappear.

The two questions for you are, where do you sit and where do you want your business to be? If you are a new business you have a great opportunity to apply the principles that we are about to present to you and to design your own future. If you are an established business you are about to read about ideas that you will be able to apply to help you grow and stay ahead by being smarter, not necessarily by having to spend more.

We include interviews with four businesses to demonstrate some of the principles in action, we chose these businesses because we had been impressed by each of them. What we discovered when we talked to them was that they all shared a common ideal and it is a key part of their success. Aligning your commercial activities with high personal and ethical standards is a huge win for everyone. Acting, fairly, kindly and responsibly is a recipe for even greater success.

We are John Wright and Ligia Turincio, together we have product and service industry experience spanning several decades, Ligia is a Mexican qualified lawyer with extensive experience in the banking sector as well as time served as a Social Media Manager. John is a marketeer by training with many years experience as a CEO as well as setting up and running businesses. Ligia and John are now both partners in the Lawbiz Consulting Group UK a business consultancy with offices in the UK and a number of Latin American countries.

We have lived the process of setting up a business from scratch and taking it to profitability and a multi-million turnover and so we know that doing this on your own with limited resources is a lonely place to be, this book has been written with that firmly in mind.

1. HOW THE BUSINESS WORLD HAS CHANGED

Things are always changing but there are some fundamental points that we should talk about first because they give perspective to much of what follows in this book.

At the time of writing 60% of the global population has access to the internet, almost 100% in developed markets and when we consider the word 'access' that means, for most people, 24/7, no (or low) cost, access. A very long way from the carefully managed and slow delivery of say a daily newspaper in the past. This seismic shift in how the world communicates has had many impacts but the key one for us to think about is that your customers have now become your boss, what they say goes.

In the old world a single customer's sphere of influence was friends and family or a letter to a supplier if they were really energised, suppliers could very easily manage this lack of transparency to their advantage; just one example of this was differential pricing, between countries, markets, branches of the same store, even individual customers.

Today we can now almost instantly find the price of anything, anywhere in the world made even easier by global sales platforms such as Amazon and Ebay. Similarly, suppliers who deliver poor products or services have nowhere to hide and the speed and ferocity of reaction can be truly terrifying.

Warren Buffet was asked for a tip for small business success and he said '*delight your customers and you will have a salesforce out there; you don't see them and you don't pay them but they are talking to people all the time*'. What a great thought. As a business owner you now have global markets, you can craft your image and present your business in any way that you choose, global transport, logistics and supply systems are so developed and intertwined that you can offer local service anywhere, you can promote yourself cheaply and effectively, anywhere. The minimal cost and speed of being able to find niche markets has never been more advantageous.

Let's dust off another old stereotypical business idea, the thinking that speed and aggression are the tools of the trade, destroying the competition, undercutting, being a little bit faster than the customer's wit, sleight of hand, winners and losers. Here, thankfully, we have seen another enormous change, many of these practises died with the arrival of the internet, no dark corners for the unscrupulous and the lazy to hide anymore, not long term anyway, but let us consider the benefits for you in this new world of transparency:

Delighting your customers as Warren Buffett suggests, what can go wrong there? You deliver what you promise, you make money, your customers are happy and they help you promote your business by telling everyone, and now we're all on line that can mean, lots and lots of '*everyone*'. We will talk in a while about over delivery and what that will do for you. These benefits are about being clever, thinking how others think, truly enjoying people being delighted by what you do for them.

The same idea applies to your employees, why not think of ways to delight them, every person in your organisation can add huge value to your business, if they wish to, if you find ways to make them want to. The jury is no longer out on this point, a sense of control of their work, a clear sense of purpose, a positive company culture, recognition, opportunities for development all rank higher than a pay rise. So the truth is that being a good guy now pays better money than being a bad one.

So please hold those thoughts in mind as we start to consider how we are going to make these powerful ideas work for you.

2. BUSINESSES ARE SIMPLE

No one ever lost money by making things simple We can almost hear the complaints as you read that sentence, how can a business be simple? If that's true then why doesn't every business succeed? Why doesn't everyone own one? Well, those are good points but take care here, we didn't say 'easy', we said 'simple'. Here's what we mean:

A successful business is one that produces goods or services that it sells for a profit which covers all the costs and leaves an acceptable return on the capital invested.

If you want to complicate this further you can, and many, if not most people in business do, but this summarises the goal, simple.

So, we are not naïve, we know that from this point there is a mass of detail to be considered to make this happen but the point here is that if everything aligns with this key principle then you will have a successful business.

The principle is so simple in fact that you're probably wondering how it's even possible to get this wrong. We will talk soon about how businesses are started and why, because the motivation can impact this hugely, but for now, here are a few of the diversions that we have witnessed that take the attention away from the principle:

'We need to get the new office and staff in place so we'll be ready for when the business comes'.

'We need to get some traction first, before we worry about profit'.

'We need everyone in the business to understand ...fill in diversion here..., before we...'.

'We need to establish ourselves as the number 1 in......'.

We are sure you could add many more but you see a common theme here, none of this kind of thinking and activity brings in cold hard cash, now, and that's the only thing that matters. Do you think we are oversimplifying again? Well, consider what makes us think like that. Would you rather develop your business from revenues, even if it takes longer, or live with the burden of debt or see your savings dwindle?

So this is what we are also trying to save you from:

Navel gazing meetings, un read minutes and bold but ultimately useless statements of intent, overly optimistic self-congratulation, lack of clarity, wasted investment. As we said at the begining, no one ever lost money by making things simple. Ok a bit of an over generalisation but we don't think we are far from the truth. Your customers are the most important people in your business life and they are complex, but their behaviours are not and the reason for this is that you are not the most important thing in their lives and so you warrant only as much of their time and attention as you are able to justify.

Perhaps this gives you an idea of what we mean:

There is a resort in Southern England with a row of shops facing the sea, a pelican crossing leads from the beach right to two ice cream shops adjacent to each other, one offers a maximum of four flavours on any one day, the other possibly 20 or 30, can you guess which has the longest queue and makes the most money? It's the one with the restricted choice, not the obvious answer is it, but here's why. Buying an ice cream is not a major decision and so people are invested, but only to a point and so the more complex the decision the more likely they are to look for an easier route be that choosing not to buy, or as in the case of the ice cream shops, the restricted range.

'Decision exhaustion' is now a term, Google anything you want and you know how many hundreds if not hundreds of thousands of results you will see, consumers want, no not just want, they crave simplicity.

The baseline truth here is that consumers want a relationship with your product or service as far as it resolves a problem for them, better and cheaper than any other solution that they can find, that's it.

The faster and easier that you can help them get to this point, the more likely they are to buy from you.

Here's another opinion on this subject for you:

'Sales at 'limited assortment' stores – a category that includes Trader Joe's, Aldi and Lidl are projected to grow 5.6% annually for the next few years, whilst sales at traditional supermarkets are projected to increase 0.5% annually.' *Source: Inmar Analytics.* It's perhaps a question of price as well but who wants to spend their time in a supermarket? Just out of curiosity we visited a main UK supermarket website and searched for 'ham', would it surprise you to learn that it yielded 62 products?

Why does this matter for you? Well think about your offer, in fact better still, get someone who knows nothing about your product or service to think about it and find out what they see.

- Is it clear what it does?
- Do they understand what problem it solves?
- Is there a need for that problem to be solved?
- Has the problem already been solved?
- Is the price clear?
- Does the name or brand help the consumer to understand, or not?
- Do they need anything else to use it (batteries, cables, bulbs etc)?

All these points are clear to you but that doesn't help because you are never going to be a customer, it's what your customers perceive that matters. Customers are busy, remember, that doesn't mean uninformed, it means that if you manage to get someone's interest they are only going to invest a small amount of time and energy trying to understand what it is you are selling. So if these, and other points are not answered clearly and immediately, you have lost your sale and they are never coming back! We will revisit all these points in detail later, but for now, let's move on.

And while we're here, think about how many products solve problems for which there is no demand or for which better solutions already exist. Who remembers New Coke from the 1980's? If you do then probably only by its' infamy, Coke was losing ground to Pepsi as Pepsi was getting attention from their Pepsi Challenge promotion, so Coke developed a product that would taste more like Pepsi, it fared well in pre-launch tests but failed miserably and was withdrawn a few weeks after launch, they had delivered a solution to a problem that never existed.

We're sure you've heard the term 'customer journey' perhaps a little over used these days but a good summary for what we do next. We will address product and service development later on, plenty to be discovered there so for the moment let's just assume that your product or service is ready to go, we are now at the beginning of the race, not the finish line.

The customer journey is the process of understanding the customer and potential customers process from not knowing you exist, to buying your product or service.

What are their thoughts, emotions and decisions at every step of the process? Understanding these and making objective decisions based on what you learn will increase your success exponentially. We are becoming repetitive now but let's not forget, customers are straightforward, unless your product or service has life changing implications it is going to be a small part of their day, a day filled with plenty of other distractions so you need to ensure that you remove any blocks to their attention or any uncertainties. As we have already discussed, the easiest way for a customer to deal with an uncertainty is to walk away.

Here are some questions that you may wish to find the answers to:

- How/when does somebody realise that they have a need for your product or service?
- How do they go about solving that need?
- How much time, money and effort will they dedicate to resolving the problem?
- Are other solutions available?
- Where do you fit into this process, how can they find what you have to offer?
- What is the customers experience of their contact with your business?
- What are the most common objections?

Know your enemy! What does a satisfied customer look like? Can you define that? You need to know this because a successful business allows you to make a profit and fulfil a need, 'win win' and also because satisfied customers will promote your business by word of mouth, and the more satisfied they are, the more likely they are to promote your product or service.

3. HOW AND WHY BUSINESSES START

There are of course many reasons but here are a few that we have come across:

You have a great new idea.

You have worked in an industry for a while and know enough to now use your expertise for your own benefit, not someone else's.

You are tired of working for someone else and being told what to do.

You want your freedom.

You want real wealth.

You wish to retire early.

Not an exhaustive list but it probably covers most motivations.

So here's a scenario for you, see if you recognise the tale, someone has a great new idea for a product, they tell all their friends about it, maybe at a dinner party, nobody wants to offend the host and the host is the great friend after all so everyone expresses support and wildly optimistic views of the future which expand with the wine consumption. Everyone needs support but 'go for it', 'I always knew you'd make it', 'we all have to take a chance now and again', 'we'll come and visit you when you make your first million', you can write the rest of the script, these are kind thoughts but all ultimately useless. Why useless? Well let's call it the X Factor effect, we're sure you've all seen talent shows where someone with supreme confidence puts on an embarrassingly bad performance displaying a clear void where talent should be and then is annoyed and surprised when the truth is pointed out to them. How does this happen? It is because their confidence comes from the continual praise that they have received from their least objective judges, friends and family; much kinder to have had some honesty long before it ran its' full and embarrassing course.

Business is an exact parallel, your friends and family are unlikely to be your customers and delightful as they all undoubtedly are, their opinions are of little help to you. The only person who will tell you the truth is someone from whom you are asking to part with money in exchange for what you are selling.

Objectivity is all. Invite the truth and pay attention to it when it arrives, this is not the time to bolster your preconceived wishes with flattery and half-truths.

You have enough experience to go it alone. Our new-found friend, objectivity should be the loudest voice here. Some people suffer a bit of resentment in long term jobs, along the lines of, 'I make all the money for this business and the boss is off playing golf/driving a shiny new car/taking multiple holidays a year.....', if this is you then of course you may have a point but let objectivity be your guide, the boss also takes the risk, pays your pension and holidays and are you going to get into an unpleasant battle over approaching customers? Are you planning to create new business or take another slice out of the same pie? If all these points have been addressed and it all still adds up then don't let our sage advice deter you but our point is, don't be emotional, make objective decisions.

We don't need to waste your time here talking about the joys and pitfalls of being your own boss, we all know that it comes with a price tag. The point we would make though is that your future in the top chair relies more on your ambitions for your new project and how you structure your business to make it all work for you. The following section explains why being a business owner can be the closest thing to slavery you will hopefully ever experience, and how to avoid that.

How to avoid being a slave to your business

Ouch, that wasn't what you wanted to hear was it! We can't throw that out there without explaining ourselves can we so let's start. As an employee you are Mr or Mrs 9 to 5, if the business fails you will lose your job but not your personal assets, as you can with a business – we tell you how to sidestep that one later on, by the way and, you go home at 5pm without a care in the world, well hopefully!

Anyway, here's a scenario that we have witnessed many times. The person who starts a business usually has an abundance of talent and energy, juggling many tasks to keep the ship afloat and crucially managing many roles early on to keep costs in check, so far so good. This gets the business underway and ensures that nothing gets missed but what happens next? The business grows and rapidly exceeds the capacity of one person to effectively manage and this is where businesses can hit a brick wall, or even fail. Two problems arrive at this point, if all decision making is still passing through one person then it all grinds to a halt, the person at the top will, unless they are unique be great at some things and not at others, so the latter category will suffer; imagine a salesperson running a company who doesn't understand finance, or vice versa. And, one person can only do so much.

So why is delegation so hard? Because the business owner knows that if he or she does everything then it will always be done to their standard, and the sort of person with the drive needed to start a business often lacks the ability to relinquish control.

The key to delegation is to give over responsibility and to avoid the temptation to interfere or criticise because as soon as you do that, the person who has been given the task will give up. They may smile to your face and say all the right things, but their heart might not truly be in it. When you delegate accept that the work may not be done in the way that you would do it but that doesn't mean that it has been done badly. If you can't live with that then keep on doing it yourself but accept that it will hinder growth.

The talented owner knows what she or he really adds to the business and what others do better, and hires the others.

Which brings us to the bit about becoming a slave to your business. Here's what we suggest for day 1 of running your new business:

Decide what you want, how long do you want to work for? Do you want to sell your business, pass it on, get someone else to run it and keep an income?

You think we're running ahead of ourselves here don't you, well bear with us for a little longer.

The more your business runs without your direct intervention in everything, the bigger and faster it can grow and the more freedom you will have. This does not mean that you lose control or interest, in fact entirely the reverse. You can be effective for a certain number of hours every day, if much of that time is doing work that others can do equally well or better then you are not using your time properly, do the stuff that only you can do and if you really want freedom, find someone that can do that too.

So where's the big idea then? Well systemise your business, make sure everything runs faultlessly when you're not there, this has two major benefits, the first is that you don't need to work inhuman hours and most importantly so that your business can be sold or passed on when you decide; who wants to buy a business that only functions with the previous owner in place. Design your business so that at any point you could hand the door key to someone else and you can be sure that the business will continue to run and deliver profits.

We have heard it said that McDonalds is, in this respect at least, the perfect business. When you buy a franchise you go to McDonalds University, you receive training and a manual and you are told that the cardinal sin is to deviate from the manual in any way. Why is this? Because the business is systemised to the extent that it delivers the same product consistently, anywhere in the world, as a customer you know precisely what you will get and what you will pay, nothing more, but nothing less either. A franchise can run perfectly well using staff with no previous experience because they are following the system. This is a very good example of the type of business that could change ownership from one day to the next without disruption or loss of revenue.

Putting systems in place is good business practise anyway, if you cannot accept and implement these points then you will be the slave of your business.

4. MEETINGS

Meetings can form such a huge part of some businesses and absorb so much resource that we think we should shine a light on them.

Meetings are a double-sided coin, run and managed correctly they assist in the smooth running of a business, but they can become a massive drain on resources with little quantifiable benefit. We feel the need to explain ourselves first as that was quite strong: To look at an unproductive meeting you first need to consider motivations, here are some:

- *I want my team around me so that I can feel empowered.*
- *I will invite absolutely everyone so that no one can say they weren't aware of the decisions made.*
- *I don't have the confidence to come to a decision so I will have a meeting to discuss the problem – note the word 'discuss', not 'resolve'.*
- *I like the sound of my own voice.*

Which leads to long meetings where everything may be carefully documented but the minutes are rarely acted upon or revisited. A personal example that we doubt is untypical was an employer who held monthly meetings for all senior managers, the meetings regularly ran for 12 hours or more, everyone took a laptop, no one spoke except the chair, the points discussed were mostly irrelevant for most of the attendees, most of the time, many attendees also spent 24 hours travelling to and from the meetings.

Imagine the lost opportunity cost of having your top team tied up plus the salary, hotel and airline costs. Enormous, unaccounted and largely unproductive expenditure that would not go unchallenged if it appeared anywhere else in a business.

The Harvard Business Review estimates that Executives spend an average of 23 hours per week in meetings and after questioning a good sample of senior managers 65% said meetings keep them from completing their own work. 71% said meetings are unproductive and inefficient. 64% said meetings come at the expense of deep thinking (see below) and 62% said meetings miss opportunities to bring the team closer together.

And one last little niggle, well a big one actually, before we move onto a more productive train of thought: Georgetown computer science professor Cal Newport uses the term 'deep thought' to describe the ability to focus without distraction on a cognitively demanding task. Crucially for this discussion, meetings interfere with that process to a significant degree.

So not exactly a ringing endorsement of the status quo but meetings are essential for enabling collaboration, creativity, and innovation. They often foster relationships and ensure proper information exchange. They provide real benefits, so what can we do?

The primary point is to be aware of the costs and benefits of meetings, they are a business tool like any other, an investment and so they should be correctly managed, follow procedures and most importantly, account for the time and financial resource that they absorb. If allowed to run their own course you run the risk of eating into the time of your most important and highly paid employees and worse still demotivating them and distracting them from constructive work.

If your operation is up and running then what follows should be very relevant, if you are a new business then you can use it to structure a way to move forwards. Here are nine ideas to help make meetings work for you:

1. Don't assume that you or anyone else is a great leader of meetings, you may be but if you can stand a bit of self-reflection please consider these points:

- ✓ Do people stay focussed? Are there side conversations?
- ✓ Do meetings stay on topic?
- ✓ Do meetings lead to firm decisions (not deferred to a committee/meeting/another day)?
- ✓ Who does all the talking?
- ✓ What seems to energise people?
- ✓ Do meetings overrun (and therefore disrupt attendees subsequent plans)?
- ✓ Can you name the positive, quantifiable benefits that came from the last two meetings, personal and corporate benefits?

2. Ask everyone how useful meetings are or are not, and how much time they take from other work, encourage absolute openness and honesty otherwise this exercise is wasted.

Discuss the results together and include and consider everyone in coming to a solution moving forwards.

Regularly review the results, as a group.

Block out meeting free times for everyone in the business.

Allow attendees to self-excuse themselves from meetings or parts of meetings if clearly irrelevant for them.

Make all meetings technology free, no mobiles or laptops.

Set an agenda and stick to it, finish at the agreed time.

And don't be afraid to change course if things aren't working, everyone respects humility.

If you want be more efficient on your time management "How to be a Time Master" by Ian Cooper is a fantastic book and dedicates a chapter to managing meetings.

5. WHAT DO CONSUMERS WANT?

We want to use this section to open some thoughts and discussion about current thinking and research. Most of the views given here take us a few steps back from the practical aspects of direct communication with our potential audiences but we would argue that understanding trends, thinking and behaviours helps shape a coherent and effective communication strategy and product offer.

These are some of the most important motivators for consumers today, they do not establish a need, more a direction of travel when a need has been identified. To explain by example, if an eco-conscious consumer has a choice of two roughly similar and equal products and one is able to boast eco credentials and one not, then it makes sense for the consumer to buy the eco offer, indeed they are likely to be happy to pay a premium for the eco version if it really matters to them.

You can craft the image that you wish to attach to your product or service and select which aspects you wish to promote but if you are able to boast about your eco or other important credentials then make sure that they are built into the DNA of your business, not tacked on at the end.

Consumers want connection.

Let's start with social media, in one way uniting and dynamic and in another highly divisive. Uniting because niche, social, interest and commercial groups can find each other and interact as friends. If for example your passion is a particular rock group, the internet allows you to join fans all over the globe, you become part of a global friendship group, sharing ideas, maybe even meeting up. Compare this to the monthly newsletter landing on peoples' doormats that must have been the way it used to work. But it's also divisive in the sense that it gives a platform and a cloak of anonymity to anyone who wishes to express an opinion on any subject at any time.

We would rather not detail examples here but we all must know cases where a point of view has drowned under a subsequent downpour of criticism and often vile abuse. Political opinion perhaps typifies the point, it's often a stark choice between left and right, you buy an ideology wholesale or not at all which fosters inclusion and exclusion and thus division.

Consumers want connection, it's in our nature and very strongly supported by research and brands, when they become influential enough brands can foster connection and social media is the number one tool. Connection brings loyalty, repeat purchase and recommendation. So what does this kind of connection actually look like? Trust in your product or service is the number one connector but closely followed by you aligning with your customers values and understanding their wants and needs and this means taking the time and being seen to genuinely engage.

Here's some research about brands from SproutSocial which gives some insights into consumer expectations from brands, so the bar is now high.

High expectations: what today's consumers want from brands

Be positive contributors to society — **72%**

Connect with their consumers — **64%**

Use their power to help people — **64%**

Bring people together toward a common goal — **49%**

Raise the moral standard for others — **48%**

Unite people from different backgrounds — **46%**

Act as leaders in our society — **43%**

sproutsocial   sproutsocial.com/brandsgetreal

Remember that the consumer is king, it helps to understand this statement by reflecting what the world was like before this was the case. Pre internet an individual consumers sphere of influence was friends and family and with less dynamic communication, probably less than a handful of people, meeting people at work or in the street, occasional 'phone calls meant that a good or bad shopping experience would not get spread too far. Of course the reverse is now the case, a fired up consumer can almost instantly broadcast across multiple channels and if the story is juicy enough it will be shared, thus increasing the spread exponentially. Great for you if the consumer loves you, a disaster if not.

But this is not all, customers also want your brand to make connections between themselves. The reasons why they believe this to be possible are neatly shown here, taken again from SproutSocial.

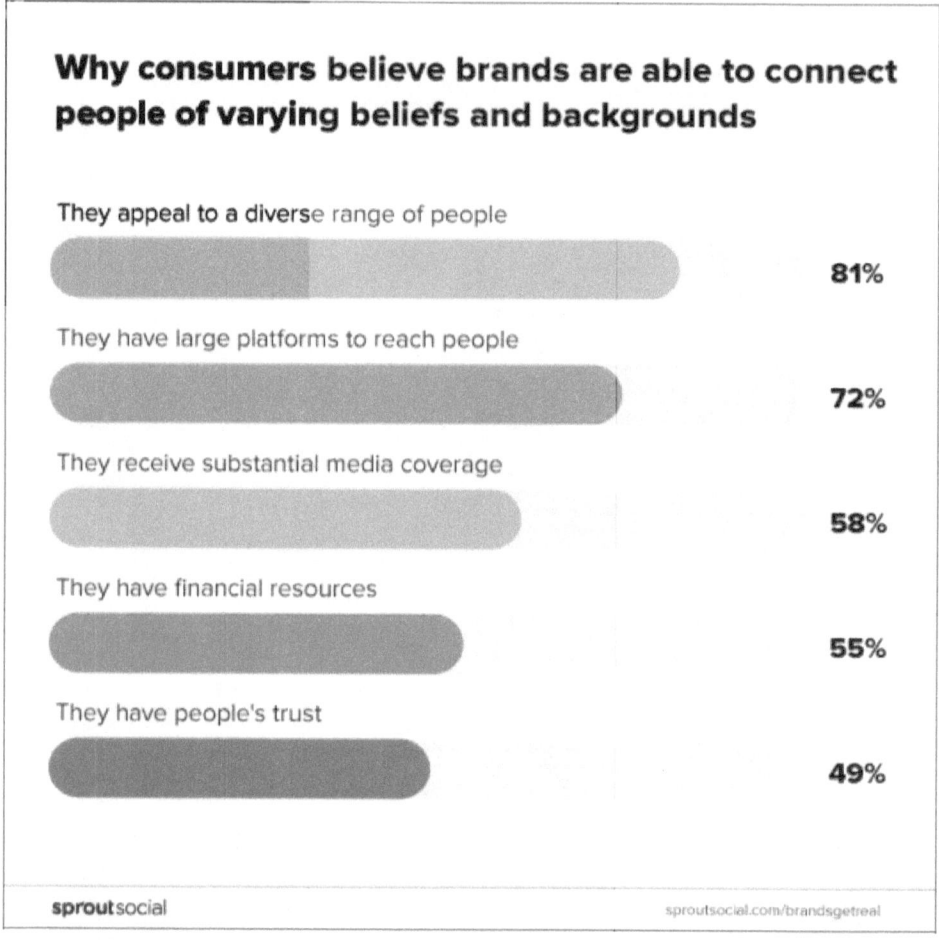

Bigger brands are almost expected to take a stance on social issues because consumers want to know who they are dealing with when they make their buying decisions, and what a thin tightrope they walk to be sincere and not appear to be cynically exploitative. These are some of the issues that brands involve themselves with, natural disasters, education, environmental, human rights, poverty and homelessness.

Clever organisations have been able to move beyond the traditional love hate relationship that many businesses have with their customers, their consumers now talk to them, they want to hear from them and they are their friends.

Do you think we are dreaming? How have they been able to jump over this barrier of distrust? Smart marketeers now use social media to relate to their customers as friends, no longer preaching and demanding, more joining in the conversation, making them laugh, being part of the party. Netflix uses its' own material to create memes, amusing, engaging and smarter still, advertising their own content at the same time.

Take a look at Wendy's the US fast food chain, who would have thought that burgers could get your attention, '*If we can't hug let's nug*' Covid 19/chicken nuggets, with a product photo', topical, part of the conversation, stepping into their customers world.

Or even more edgy, look at this Twitter exchange later posted on Instagram too:

Punchy and amusing responses, entertaining, self-deprecating content makes corporations one of the crowd rather than some faceless, money grabbing mega corporation.

People like people

Companies are faceless organisations and so humanising your product or service will enormously increase your ability to connect. Products and services are of interest to consumers, it is of course the reason why you are communicating in the first place, but if you wish to start making connections then the people behind the product are a great story for you.

Decide the image that you wish to attach to your product or service, which should be a true reflection of reality, and craft the human stories that you wish to use to connect with your customers.

Consumers use products to express their values

You may not like what's coming next but it's a reality, consumers and most particularly younger consumers, think of themselves as their own brand. This operates at two levels, firstly consider the time, posing and sometimes Photoshop hours that go in to some peoples' online imagery, would you dare share someone's image online without running it past them first? If you are a parent of teenage children you will know exactly what we are talking about. If you live in an online world then your image is even more of an expression of you and your values than you being in front of someone in person; your look can be, and is, dissected, you are likely express a broader range of opinions and personal facts than you would in a conversation. The second level at which this operates is self-marketing online as a way of making money, do we really believe that some of the dumbed down personalities that we can see on line are actually a true reflection of that person, we really doubt it, but the dumbed down version attracts attention and income. Where products and services touch this weird new world, their image is absolutely key because the message is strong and if the image does not fit the story being told, it will have been discarded long before.

But this runs a lot deeper than the here today, gone tomorrow fads of youth, think about some of the other more impactful subjects discussed, eco values, local sourcing, carbon neutral, diversity and equality. These are all worthy causes and if your business has a social agenda as well as a commercial one then some or all of these are probably in the DNA of your business but consumers want to know where and how you touch these subjects and where you sit. It is a huge opportunity both to do something useful with your business and to align yourself with important social values.

But it really helps if you mean it!

What is the difference between 'jumping on a bandwagon' for commercial advantage and really having an agenda for social justice in your business? We think we can all spot the difference between the two but maybe struggle to define it.

Here are a couple of examples that passed under our noses, coming in to a rail station recently all the signage was rainbow themed, did we really believe that the rail company has an agenda in support of LBGT rights beyond their legal obligations, perhaps, but maybe also an organisation exploiting an issue for assumed commercial gain. A different example where the commitment is perhaps clearer is Ecoboard a manufacturer of eco surfboards, traditional surfboards use a lot of toxic and non-recyclable materials that break down in the oceans if discarded, the whole basis of the Ecoboard business is to resolve this problem with a viable eco friendly alternative, our point being that where a key social value is built into the fabric of the business, indeed it has been founded on this ethos, there is no cynicism or argument and so if eco credentials matter to you, and you surf, what will you do next?

People want others to know what they stand for and if your product or service can help them then you have a big advantage but it is a very fine line to tread and consumers can sniff out insincerity in an instant. And of course the reverse is true, here's another example from the surf world. Surfers Against Sewage is an influential and respected organisation with a clear agenda very adequately summarised in the name and it acts for anyone who loves the sea, you don't only need to surf. Here is a recent headline from them which has been widely shared:

> *'Today, Surfers Against Sewage (SAS) has revealed that Coca-Cola is the worst polluter out of 207 brands and responsible for 15 per cent*

> *of all plastic waste they recorded.'*

Would you want to see your name here? If you were Coca-Cola what would you do? How much of this do they need to see before they act? A huge global brand versus a small eco charity, probably they're not losing too much sleep right now but these narratives have a habit of growing very fast, and particularly where the subject touches a lot of people's core values.

Our, admittedly, anecdotal view is that consumers have an in-built mistrust, almost a resentment of large corporations and any cause that draws attention to corporate wrong doing, or perceived wrong doing, is never going to lack supporters.

Social responsibility -Intercam Banco

To demonstrate the importance of putting the values that your customers identify with in the DNA of your business, we interviewed Eduardo García Lecuona, Chairman of the Board of Intercam Banco. Intercam has been recognised as a Socially Responsible Company by the Mexican Centre for Philanthropy and the Alliance for Corporate Social Responsibility in Mexico.

Intercam Banco is a Mexican bank with a strong commitment to social responsibility, we spoke to Eduardo Garcia Lecuona, President of Intercam to find out how this had come to be part of the business and why. This is what he had to tell us.

> 'I started my career in corporate banking and when I decided to set up my own business as a Foreign Exchange Broker I faced the problem of finding a way to connect with corporate contacts, as a small business. I found that the answer was personal relationships but I also soon discovered that I was not the key ingredient for every dish, different people connect with other different people and so for me the road to diversity began by hiring wide ranging people. So what began as a business strategy became a business purpose, you cannot go against your nature. I started the business with what I call three pieces of luck, or maybe three guiding lights, ethical principles,

my father made me understand that doing the right thing was the only option, very hard work and focus, not getting side lined. So Intercam has made money every year since 1987, even during the more turbulent times. Giving back is personally satisfying, it needs to be to make someone want to keep on doing it but it is also a part of being grateful and thankful, so it became a part of what we do. In the beginning it was haphazard, without a plan, so I organised a committee to decide on which causes and who to give to.

Of course this activity must benefit the business, we make sure people know what we are doing, we want our customers, the regulators and other interested parties to see what we are and who knows, maybe it might even inspire a competitor to start or increase their giving. Besides this there are three main benefits, firstly our employees appreciate working for a good company and feeling good about their employer.

Secondly, our customers see us through different eyes. And thirdly, we and our shareholders feel good about ourselves too. Here are three practical examples of how we have applied this, after the earthquake in Mexico City in 2017 a friend mentioned that her restaurant was giving 400 free meals a day to Doctors and Nurses, we donated too, but we also invited our staff and customers to contribute and matched their giving peso for peso, increasing the donations to 1200 meals a day for 90 days.

During the same disaster myself, my wife and 400 Intercam employees went to a devastated town in Mexico State and built seven houses for homeless people, we all got tired and dirty and the people fed us and what a satisfying experience it was. We have 30 branches in tourist areas and from time to time our employees go out and clean the beaches and they love the experience too. So social responsibility is truly a cornerstone of Intercam, we want to benefit financially as well as in the many other ways explained here and for the causes we support to benefit, it's a win win and nobody gains by us being modest'.

Consumers want to take care of themselves

This can be seen in the growth of fitness, wellness and diet and all the associated, app's, products, courses, books, videos etc, can you think of anyone you know who does not interact with one or more of these? How would you have answered the same question ten years ago? Have you heard of JOMO? 'The joy of missing out', Euromonitor identified this consumer driver which refers to the pleasure in spending time alone or resting. Social media is increasingly seen as an obligation, 'I haven't had time to look at my messages today, I'll get on with it later', does that sound familiar? Social media has also become a task to be escaped from on occasions.

Consumers are now the experts

What do you do when you want to buy a new product or service? Manufacturers websites are part of the discovery process but most of us now turn to forums, reviews and the opinions of other consumers before we make a decision. If the reviews are all 5 star how much more convincing do you find that than all the praise on the website? Other consumers have stood in our shoes and then handed over their money, how did the story roll out from there? Harnessing and encouraging the good feedback and counteracting the bad (everyone gets bad feedback sometimes), is an essential business skill today, ignore it at your peril. Suppliers now pay for consumers to promote their product or service, we originally used the word 'bribe' rather than 'pay' and thought it perhaps a little pejorative but we think the experience properly sits between the two. If an influencer is given free products for an online review then the review is going to positive is it not? A negative review will stem the flow of free products. Clearly followers will need to have strong confidence in the integrity of reviewers for their opinions to be of value.

Consumers are getting fed up with plastics, want to see sustainability and kindness to animals Not long ago we came home from the supermarket and unpacked the fruit and vegetables, the pile of plastic was bigger than the fruit and vegetables, yes we could have compacted the packaging but let's not get pedantic here, there's a much more important point to be made. For our household this prompted the move to a local fruit and vegetable supplier with loose stock and paper bags, are we particularly virtuous? We don't think so. We see the plastic islands in the oceans, tread across it on the beach, there is a growing feeling that something needs to be done and that we all need to 'do our bit'.

The historical industrial model takes resources, processes them and then discards the waste and eventually discards the product too, to waste, the imperative is entirely commercial with no thought given to any of the many unwanted consequences. It seems so antiquated now doesn't it. The circular view of production considers the human, ethical and environmental consequences of the activity at each stage with the end game being the reuse of everything in the process. Nirvana maybe, but social pressure has forced even the most unwilling to take steps towards sustainable production and this pressure will continue to increase. The consumer is now king, do you remember that? If you don't respond to consumer wishes you cannot keep it a secret for long and the fallout will be expensive. But great news if you are a new or young business, you can design your business around these principles and shout it to the world.

Sustainable products - Authentic House

We wanted to have some thoughts from a company founded with sustainability built into the very fabric of the business and so we spoke to Alice Ojeda founder of Authentic House. Authentic House is an online store and eco-friendly subscription box selling sustainable, plastic-free home and beauty products, the company started trading in 2018. Here's what Alice Ojeda had to tell us.

'The idea for Authentic House came when I was exploring ways that I could build a social enterprise that would help people create an eco-friendly home. The name 'Authentic House' came from the idea that a home should reflect and be authentic to the values that the occupants wishes to live by. The strategy has been to empower more people to live sustainably and to make a positive impact in the world.

I began by interviewing experts in all aspects of eco-friendly homes – from architects to cabinet makers and product designers. Eventually, I came across two products that I had never seen before. One was a dish brush made of coconut husk fibres and the other was a hand-sewn washing up sponge. Both products were inherently beautiful, simple and far better for the planet than an average plastic brush and sponge.

I was familiar with the subscription box model and loved the surprise of receiving new products in the post each month, but I eventually fallen out of love with the waste and unused products it created. I thought I could create a different kind of subscription box, with purpose, that would send people eco-friendly products to enjoy at home and in this way help them make small, positive changes every month.

The UN has set out its Sustainable Development Goals as a blueprint for creating a better future. Our focus is on goal 12: 'Responsible Production and Consumption.' This means we focus on our customers first, always offering only ethically sourced and plastic-free goods, or the best alternatives at the time. We keep our margins as low as we can, without compromising on quality, because we want to make eco-friendly alternatives as accessible as possible.

As we grew, I accepted that reducing our plastic waste is not the only measure we need to take to protect the planet and that climate change is a pressing issue. Starting in 2019, we began to make donations for every subscription box sent to plant trees in the UK. Recently, we've extended this to plant a tree for every order or subscription made, because I feel it's important for people to know the impact their choices are making. We'll be planting these trees across the world to create mixed, native woodland.

Maintaining our eco integrity is of course important for example when sourcing products, we'll ask how the product helps to reduce waste or minimise environmental impact, or whether it supports craftspeople or a minority group. Where a product contains plastic, we'll only accept this if the plastic has no alternative and if it's the best option for a product that will last a long time. If we sell a product, it needs to have a function and not be purely decorative or a 'greenwashed' replacement of a perfectly viable product most people have. For example, we don't stock bamboo cutlery.

To manufacture our Authentic House products, we work closely with craftspeople in the UK and occasionally source from abroad. The majority of the brands we source from are female-owned and increasingly we're looking to support BAME (Black, Asian and Minority Ethnic) owned businesses too.

The majority of our customers are women and of a wide range of ages (from 25 to around 60). Our typical customer is educated and cares about protecting the environment. They shop with us because we reflect their values and they can trust that any product we will offer is envir-

onmentally friendly and ethically made.

I think that anyone who is making an effort to purchase sustainably now is an early adopter in the growth curve of this movement. We're the people who are willing to spend time learning about new options and even to pay a little more for a product without the underlying environmental cost. As this movement grows, I believe that purpose-led businesses will come to the forefront and those businesses that don't contribute to our communities will face pressure to change or become irrelevant. Already we can see larger brands such as Aldi and Primark creating new 'eco-friendly' ranges. We have all seen through the global pandemic and climate change, how fragile our existence is. I don't think change will happen immediately, but I think inevitably soon it'll be unthinkable to purchase or offer any other product than one which respects other humans, nature and our planet'.

Consumers want to be streamlined.

We talked about simplicity and clarity before, streamlining is part of this process. Connectivity and ease of communication are the norm' now, the baseline, not something to be attained. The more consumers can enjoy simplicity in satisfying their needs the more they can feel in control. Products or services that streamline and simplify will enjoy consumer support.

Consumers like 'unique'

We've all done mass produced, 'unique' brings together a number of points already presented here. The need for products and services to be a reflection of a consumers view of themselves, to support themselves as a 'brand'. We are all unique and most of us have a need to express and enjoy that fact. We all like a story, a talking point, unique products and services give consumers that, make it interesting enough and they will promote your business in a way that you could never have dreamed about. It's also sometimes a question of status, better quality, differentiated products allow consumers to feel good about themselves, and dare we say it, yes perhaps superior too.

Young is the new old

The 50+ market is growing in number and proportion worldwide, they are wealthier, healthier and living longer. For the main part these people don't want to slide gracefully into their dotage, they want to run, cycle, travel, eat out, climb mountains, go to the gym..... in just the same way that their children do, in this sense the older generation behave in the same way as their children and they have money to spend and a disregard for their age.

Inclusion and compassion mean a lot

Marginalised groups and their supporters have become more and more vocal and products and services that genuinely take the challenges presented and address them sincerely will be kindly regarded. Large retailers such as Tommy Hilfiger and Target offer clothes for children with particular sensory, mobility or medical needs, care has been taken maintain aesthetics and pricing in line with the more mass-market offerings.

Consumers need to be right

The need for human beings to be right, to feel that they are a little better informed, to be doing the right thing, is a hugely strong driver of behaviour. We selected the word 'need' here with some care, the drive is far stronger than 'prefer' or 'want'.

This comment has pleasant and unpleasant connotations, being right in your behaviour towards others is kind, loving and empowering, being right for the sake of crushing someone is not. If you are unsure about this statement then just read product reviews, many are so ludicrously uninformed but the internet gives the platform for us all to be 'experts' and we are all confident enough in our opinions to use it very liberally. From a marketing viewpoint, tapping into this drive can be beneficial, giving your customers some of the benefits that they are asking for allows them to feel good about themselves, think about our buying fruit and vegetables in paper bags, we get a little buzz of self-satisfaction every time we put away the shopping without all that plastic waste.

6. LET'S TALK ABOUT YOUR OFFER

You need to be bigger, better, faster, more appealing than your competitors and you would like to do it with little or no investment, are we right about that?

Let's start with your product or service and then we can move on to how to get ahead, smartly, not expensively.

Product development

You may already have a product or service or you may be looking to develop something new, in either case there is something to think about here.

Here are some thoughts if you want inspiration to start from scratch:

- ✓ You could update something that already exists, an eco version of a successful product or a better version of a service.
- ✓ You could find another use for an existing product, for example, could liquid bathroom soap work as a pet shampoo?
- ✓ You could find a new route to market, the internet is ideal for this, how many fortunes have already

been made by disruptors to traditional industries using the internet, think about glasses, wine and food, books, music...

- ✓ Find complementary products or services for good selling lines.
- ✓ Adapt something to improve it or give it another use.

The following points apply to both new and existing products and services:

Is it clear what your product or service does?

This may sound obvious but we have seen many manufacturers so involved with their products that they make unreasonable assumptions about what potential consumers understand.

'No one ever lost money by making things simple', remember that? Perhaps this is this phrases' finest moment, potential consumers are smart and well informed but they will only dedicate as much time as it takes to understand what you are offering them and if your product or service doesn't explain itself immediately, they will move on.

Here is the wording from an advertisement that we saw on the back of a van recently 'Desire, Achieve, Succeed', what do you think? A motivational speaker? A gym maybe? We were intrigued so we overtook, that didn't help much either but we saw a web address and following that we discovered that we had been following a heating engineer, whoever would have guessed that! Some companies seem to use their marketing to hide what they do, nothing is more important than clarity.

Do they understand what problem your product or service solves?

This is a broader question than it sounds, is the need obvious or are you breaking new ground? If the latter then you will need to work harder because you will have to educate first and then sell. The second aspect is, does the answer to this question jump out and hit your prospective customer between the eyes within the first few seconds? How often have you seen a product or promotion for a product or service where you are really trying hard to understand what they are trying to say? Here we go again, simplicity, clarity. How does the confusion creep in? It's usually because the manufacturer, or more often the marketing department gets so engulfed in their own hype that they forget who they are talking to. Customers are smart, informed people but they only have as much time for you as you justify, yes we know we're repeating ourselves but this point is so important and so often ignored.

Is there a need for that problem to be solved?

Does this one surprise you? It would be very exciting to invent a faster, automated bottle opener for example but when has this actually ever been a problem? Is anyone out there looking for it?

Has the problem already been solved?

The answer to this is yes, no or partly and yes and partly are not the end of the road. If there is already a solution, the challenge becomes coming up with a better alternative but it does mean that the problem and solution are already understood in the market.

Is the price clear?

Does this sound a bit too obvious? Supermarkets know why this matters so much, if there is a hint of confusion then the next best offer gets the sale. The issue becomes a broader one when the offer is multi layered, you buy a base product or service and then add extras and options. Consider how the airlines and car rental companies use this to their advantage, the customer is given the headline price almost immediately because the airline or rental company knows that the decision is all but made at this point, the game then becomes how much can the supplier add between this point and the actual purchase, without the customer getting weary and going elsewhere. First on board, seat selection, food and drink, entertainment, baggage, travel insurance, cars, hotels.

Some products and services in particular will be very careful about committing to a price too early, this is for one of two reasons or possibly both. Firstly because they want to build the desire to the point that the customer has no objections left and will certainly pay whatever is asked. The second is the premium caché of 'if you need to ask the price you can't afford it', there are customers for whom including themselves in this perceived exclusive bracket is a benefit that they are happy to pay for.

Does the name or brand help the consumer to understand, or not? There is a large industry devoted to sorting out this issue and precisely because trade and brand names can have such a devastatingly good, or bad influence on the success of a product or service. There are two scenarios here:

1. The brand or trading name is already in existence; you may have acquired it. You still need to answer the questions above but overlaid with a view as to the market value of a brand that may have been promoted and understood for a long time. In other words, it may not have the best association with the product or service but if customers know the brand then the brand takes precedence, it may be the result of many years of marketing investment. To give you an example some years ago the owner of probably the best-known children's colour brand decided to ditch the rather antiquated brand name in favour of something contemporary to bring it up to date. The brand had been in existence for over 200 years and exported worldwide and so the change added nothing and left confusion in its' wake and a subsequent return to the original.

2. You are starting from scratch. This is rather like going to a party where you don't know anyone, you can be whoever you want to be. It's a blank sheet of paper and you can create a brand or trade name that reflects the image that you have decided best represents your offer. We will explore this process a little further on.

Brand and trade name protection is essential before you start to use either, in many countries it is a relatively cheap and simple process and it should be undertaken for every market that you intend to sell in. This comment applies whether you have a new or established brand (which has not been protected). This ensures that you are not about to infringe anyone else's rights and also gives you the confidence that your investment in establishing and promoting your brand or trade name cannot be nullified by someone latterly challenging your rights. Brands can have considerable commercial value as 'non-tangible assets' as well as being the driver of business.

Do they need anything else to use it?

This comes back to simplicity and clarity once again, leave your customers in any doubt and they won't buy. If they need to buy an accessory to make your product work make it as clear as soon as you can so it becomes part of the initial decision making and purchasing process. You will not be easily forgiven if you let your customer get home and find out that they need to go out, yet again, to get what they need to make the product work; the inconvenience will outweigh the additional cost by a very large margin and this is what your customers will share with their friends.

Research

This is where the internet becomes your very best friend, finding out what is out there, what it is selling for and what everybody else is doing has never been easier or more dynamic.

If your idea is a good one then it is likely that someone else is offering it or something similar, don't feel disheartened, it confirms that you are on the right track and gives you a good baseline on which to improve. Seeing what your competitors are selling, where and for how much allows you to start thinking about what you can add to make your offer more attractive.

Once you have exhausted the internet, (is that ever going to be possible!) Time to start your qualitative research, the more opinion based, less quantifiable but just as important bit. If you have customers already, what do they think of your competitors, contact your competitors through their websites and see how you are treated.

Through all this create a list of what you can do better than others. If you are entering a crowded market this exercise should climb higher up your list of priorities.

Prototyping

The prototyping phase during product development is the creation of a finished product to use as a sample for market testing and production. The process often involves experimenting with several versions of your product, slowly eliminating options and making improvements until you feel satisfied with a final version. For market testing it is also a useful process for presenting different versions in particular where design is a key element in the products' appeal. Prototyping also differs significantly depending on the type of product you are developing. The least expensive and simplest cases are products that you can prototype yourself, such as food recipes and some cosmetic products. Injection moulded plastics, technical innovations and 3D designs will require investment. Of course your own training and skills can save time and money if applicable to the process, or you will otherwise need to outsource.

Art and design colleges have students and expertise in very wide ranging disciplines and are often very interested to work with industry for their students to work on real projects not just theoretical ideas. Students may lack work life experience but they often retain an impressive ability to think laterally before having been touched by the 'been there, done that' mentality. This resource can help your product design and development as well as branding, packaging and web design. An additional benefit is that you are getting the chance to work with up and coming talent whom you may wish to offer a position to later, if you have the need.

Sourcing

Now is the time to start building your supply chain and making sure that it all works together. If you are a start-up you have no trading history and you need to establish your credibility with suppliers. Everyone welcomes new business but your relationship with your suppliers gets tested when problems arise, if there are, for example, supply problems it is logical that the supplier will protect his or her own interests first and that means he will look after the bigger clients and the best payers. So you need to get up the suppliers list of priorities as far and fast as you can, how do you do this?

- Be honest and open from the start, share your plans and vision.
- Give realistic timescales and forecasts and aim to improve on or exceed forecasts by 10%, everyone likes extra business and 10% more is likely to be manageable.
- Pay your supplier on time, never make your supplier call you to ask for money.
- If problems arise pick up the 'phone, don't wait for it to ring.
- Negotiate by all means but be reasonable, if you squeeze too hard someone will supply but you need your business to be important to them, win/win generally keeps everyone much happier and you will have a more compliant friend if you ever need a faster order, a bigger order or whatever favour you need to pull in.

Have back up suppliers in place

At this stage you should consider your complete supply chain so do not forget storage, shipping and warehousing and again think through what you will do if any of these fail.

Finding multiple suppliers for the different components and services that you will need, as well as different potential manufacturers, will allow you to compare costs. The process of sourcing several options should be seen as an essential one as it will be an important part of safeguarding your business in the long term. If you need convincing take a few minutes after you have looked fully into costing, to calculate the losses you could suffer with even minor delays or disruptions in your supply chain. You may wish to even go so far as to look at the financial strength of suppliers who will become a key part of your business, their problems can very quickly become your problems too.

How to find suppliers

The internet puts you in touch with the world, you can visit local suppliers and rely on faster deliveries but overseas ones may offer big advantages, better costs and/or quality but beware language barriers, no small matter sometimes when linguistic misunderstanding or even cultural differences or assumptions can lead to big problems. Here's a quick review of the pros and cons:

Local supply:

- Faster delivery
- You can visit to check quality before shipping and if issues arise.

Overseas supply:

- Often cheaper but slower delivery.
- Language and cultural differences can lead to misunderstandings.
- Currency fluctuations can dent or improve your margin significantly.
- Remember that your supply delay must include manufacturing, packing, and shipping time plus local clear-

ance and delivery. It is not unknown for suppliers to quote the manufacturing time only, when asked to quote availability.

- Be clear who is paying for shipping and clearance, 'fob' or 'free on board' is common parlance and means that the supplier will get it to a specified point of exit in the suppliers' country at their cost, all costs after this are then for you to pay.
- Consider import tariffs and taxes if applicable.
- Non-tariff barriers can also trip you up, such as labelling and health and safety regulations, compliance and certification should be considered well in advance.

On the face of it the overseas supplier route seems like just too much trouble but don't let us leave you with that impression, more work yes but once procedures and systems are understood and in place they don't need to be continually revisited and the added margin that you might be able to enjoy jumps straight to your bottom line.

Personal contacts are always a good start if this applies to you, by which we mean if you know someone who can recommend a supplier then you have a head start which works both ways, personal recommendation establishes initial trust and credibility.

Trade shows are still popular in some industries, a quick way for you the buyer to meet a lot of potential buyers face to face, see what they have to offer and begin to develop relationships.

Government agencies. Most countries have commercial representation based in the home country and in key overseas markets, their remit is to represent their country in overseas markets and develop two-way trade. The level and type of support varies significantly from country to country but at its' best you might get country advice, direct contacts, import/export advice, help with finding finance, inclusion in trade missions and help with research, much free of charge or often low cost.

Costing and pricing

Now is the time to sharpen your pencil and bury yourself in the numbers, you probably realised a little while ago that at least some 'back of the envelope' calculations were needed to guide your progress and discussions. Before we go any further can we remind you of this from right back at the beginning:

A successful business is one that produces goods or services that it sells for a profit which covers all the costs and leaves an acceptable return on the capital invested.

So this is inevitably where all the previous activity leads and where everything should now come together and make sense. You need to reconcile two competing forces here, your costs and what the market wants to pay for your product whilst making sure that you make enough money to run your business and make an acceptable profit.

So now think back to the market and competitor research that you undertook, you should have a good idea of what your product will sell for in the market, we put this all together and you now know how much margin you have; it is never enough so now is the time to squeeze here and adjust there to bring yourself to, hopefully, where it all adds up. If this is all new to you, we include a simple example below, some people understand better with numbers, some with words, but just before we get to that here's another thought for you:

At this point you may well have committed many hundreds of hours of work but if you have undertaken all this properly you now really know where you are, if that is not the place that you want to be, if there is unacceptable risk, if you cannot command sufficient margin, going back and restarting or abandoning the project all together may be a sensible decision. If you have to give up at this point then you have lost a few gambling chips and you will in all likelihood have another chance, objectivity is all, emotion is not.

7. OVER DELIVERY, MARKETING GOLD - HOW TO MAKE YOUR CUSTOMERS LOVE YOU

Customers are simple, their expectations by now should be clear to you, if you are selling them a pencil it must, write, sharpen without breaking, last a reasonable time be reasonably priced etc… you get the idea. So if you, the supplier, fulfil your side of the deal by complying with the above then you have done what you have been paid for, you don't warrant any special praise, but you DO want to warrant special praise, in fact you need it and to do that you have to give them something to praise you about and that means that you need to be exceptional.

To use the pencil analogy you need to figure out how to make buying a pencil from you will make your customer tell others about the experience. OK easier to do when you are selling cars rather than pencils but the principle is the same.

Give your customer more than he or she expects and you immediately become different, make that difference big enough and you become exceptional.

Here's what over delivering will do for you:

- Referrals, if you over deliver then you are much more likely to be referred, this is the cheapest way to get new customers.
- Your customers will talk about you if you give them a story to tell, who doesn't like a story?
- In the days before the internet the supplier was king, your exposure was one point of sale or one purchase, now with everything on line, the customer is king with unlimited access to information.
- Over delivery is your cheapest and most effective form of marketing.

Let's take a deeper look at these four ideas.

Think about the cost of recruiting new customers, what is the cost of social media, marketing expertise, advertising, sales representation, entertaining and/or whatever other means you use, add it all up and divide the total by the number of new customers you got last year, that gives you the cost of acquiring a new customer. If you are a new business you have to make assumptions, but the principle is the same. Now consider the cost of over delivering. What you don't know is what the return is from over delivering but that can be managed and adjusted as experience dictates; the big advantage is that you can see very immediately what you are, or are not, getting for your investment. And better still, the cost comes out of a small reduction in your margin, this is not up-front investment that you may or may never see again whether or not it generates a sale, you already have the sale.

Over delivery in the hotel industry

To demonstrate a practical example of over delivery we interviewed Mr Matías Hidalgo the Operations Director of Helios Hotels in Spain, we had stayed at the Helios Hotel in Almuñécar and had seen what over delivery looks like and so we were interested to hear how this is achieved in a service industry. Here is what Matías Hidalgo explained to us:

> 'Customer service is a science not an art and a key principle for us is to have a five star philosophy in the three star hotel, when I see luxury cars parked outside the front of the Helios I know we have achieved our aim. To implement this we have three things that we must get right, product, service and our reputation online.
>
> Communication and training are key and the daily staff meeting ensures that everyone knows their part, staff/customer ratios, occupancy rates, consistent meal standards etc. We host many events, these are managed like a play, every actor in the performance knows their part.
>
> Customers see added value in the things that we give them but don't charge for, such as a clean hotel, the hotel is continuously cleaned by our housekeeping team 18 hours per day, a well maintained building, good food and a professional, cordial and caring approach to customers. We talk to the customers and want to hear what they have to say. Connection with our clients makes them feel special and enables them to feel at home. Our one principle objective is to make the customer happy, anything that doesn't fit with that is a waste of time'.

We asked Mr Hidalgo how does he measure success:

> 'There are three variants, Repeat guests, occupancy rates with average prices compared to those of the competition, and a good online reputation. I have met many

> *General Managers who dismiss negative reviews as being fake comments written by competitors or similar unwarranted activity. This may be true in one or two cases in every thousand, but the rest are genuine. We pay attention to feedback, as it is our opportunity to improve. In the last four years the Helios Hotel rating has risen from 8.1 to 9.3 on booking.com. We have also achieved a score of 94% through 4400 comments on Trustyou.com, a site that aggregates all online reviews. On top of that we are number 1 in the region on Tripadvisor. For me, customer feedback is far more valuable than a star rating. It is possible to have a five star experience at a three star hotel or a three star experience in a five star hotel. The customer's voice doesn't lie'.*

Give them a story. We've all read statistics about how satisfied customers tell so many of their friends and dissatisfied customers so many more, well who knows the accuracy of the detail but we all know that the principle is entirely correct. Everyone loves to enthral an audience with a good story, and we all like to be amused. So how do you attach a story to your product and service? The answer is that you do something remarkable, what can you add to your offer that will make absolutely sure that the recipient tells everyone about it. Let's propose a few crazy ideas to make the point, you sell someone a new car and have the keys delivered by a knight on horseback, you buy a packet of biscuits and get given a free jelly at the till, you book a holiday and get a day trip in a glider, a bit off the wall perhaps but you see the point here, if any of these things happened to you, you'd tell everyone wouldn't you. How many people did you tell the last time you got a promotional pen?

If you like this idea and want to expand your thinking in this direction, we can recommend the book The Purple Cow, an easy read and a much more expansive explanation of this process.

The internet is your best friend and your worst enemy. Back in the days of pre-history you had your products stocked in a shop, if there was a problem with your product the shopkeeper would find out as would his or her customers, but no one else, there was no medium for sharing information widely. This allowed the supplier to very effectively manage products and prices to their advantage, the problem for suppliers was communication, with no direct dialogue with the consumer the message often got diluted from supplier to customer and the various points in the distribution chain could add their own personal bias and view; we have seen good products not listed because the owners daughter didn't like the colour! Today the customer is in charge, your pricing is transparent whether you like it or not and with on line reviews and ratings about absolutely everything, everybody sees everything. But this is a great thing because it keeps poor operators out of the market and most importantly suppliers now have a direct discourse with their consumers.

What does over delivery look like? It can be something extra in the pack, product or voucher, it can be promising three day delivery and getting it there the next day, it can be your theatre tickets coming in a gold envelope rather than a brown one, a free glass of prosecco when you are welcomed at a restaurant, a follow up call post purchase. The wackier the better, the aim is to get noticed and to get your customers to love you. It takes a little imagination that's all, but the overwhelming business benefits can vastly exceed the actual cost.

And it doesn't stop here, you can over deliver at every point of contact that the customer has with your business. Here are some ideas to expand the idea a little but you will quickly come to ideas that suit your business:

- Email enquiries, immediate response is the number 1 and can be automated to handle the delay before a personal response is possible but why not add some pictures, video, interesting product information, special offer, something of value, but given free. Something that your customer might really want.

- Complaints, there's a whole book to be written on this subject but this is the most fertile ground for giving a generous and personal response, the customer has actually taken the time to contact you rather than ditching your product and complaining about you to their friends, what better opportunity to make them feel glad that they spoke to you.

- Customer service, what kind of calls do you get/do you expect to get? Again number 1 is to pick up the 'phone within a few rings or call back promptly and before you say you will. What can you give them? Avoid trying to sell them something else, this technique has been overused beyond the point of irritation, give them something that you don't have to and that they don't expect.

8. MARKETING TRENDS THAT YOU SHOULD KNOW ABOUT

Markets and consumer behaviours are constantly changing and providing challenges and the pace of change has never been faster. If you know where the world is moving, you can move with it, stay ahead of your competitors and not miss opportunities.

The world is now online, of course we all know that but how many companies pay lip service to this new world rather than putting it at the centre of their business. Here is an example that we saw recently, a wine company sent out a teaser ad', a plate with two different looking bunches of grapes, which was the wine grape? The teaser was to highlight an offer for a discount on wine, within minutes the comments started a discussion about the actual grape variety and its' merits for certain wines, someone else had used a wine app' to point out that the quoted pre-discount wine price was actually double the market price so the quoted discount, wasn't really a discount, not a happy outcome for the wine company. What we aim to demonstrate with this anecdote is that you need an online presence and to be active online but to underestimate the power of it or the skills needed to manage it can be a fatal error. The better news is though, that correctly managed you can craft your online presence to work for your business, we are about to take you through some ideas that can help you decide how to position your business.

The pace of change is very fast, most of the business world is being left behind or playing catch up. Don't ever think you are too new, too old, too small or too anything else, you need to be on board. Major corporations have the resources to lead the way and we will reference some good examples.

Here is a summary of some current trends. Some of these ideas may well strike a chord with you now, some may be a step too far for where you are today, but understanding how things are evolving will allow you to build your business for when these things become relevant for you.

Simplicity

You may be tired of hearing this mantra but this is of course one of the main points of this book, so bear with us whilst we expand this idea further. The diffusion of information is now so cheap, easy and efficient that it is an overcrowded space, every layer of complexity that you add to your offer either hides it a little more or decreases the chance of a potential buyer giving you the time that you need to talk to them.

A good example is Apple, with that one word or that one logo, we all know what to expect, state of the art technology that anybody can use, premium priced but consumers are happy to pay more for products that look good and work. What Apple has done in essence is to engineer products that contain hugely complex technologies but to present the salient features in a language that anyone can understand and, in a product, stripped of all unnecessary buttons, knobs, switches and start up processes, simplicity.

For some groups of consumers simplicity has a philosophical appeal beyond product design too, think local sourcing, removal of non-recyclable components, clarity, back to basics, the rejection of over consumption as a logical response to a greener, healthier world.

Local purchasing and eco-authentic

We are all aware of the global pressures for manufacturers to take these issues seriously and most consumers now actively want 'to do their bit', a great opportunity for small and start up businesses to invent or reinvent themselves with these credentials in place. Many countries now have net zero carbon targets enshrined in law, the regulatory pressure coming from governments down to businesses can only increase. The UK government for example has announced that in 10 years time, petrol and diesel cars will be prohibited. That is a huge societal change.

The advantages of local purchasing are reduced carbon footprint by the reduction in transport costs, the creation of wealth in the community and the consequent strengthening of community cohesiveness. Consumers can flag wave their own support for these causes by actively buying locally, it gives a feeling of satisfaction of having done the right thing as well as being a personal statement.

Eco authentic purchasing has the same drivers, the feeling of satisfaction from satisfying a need with minimal damage to the environment as well as being a strong statement. The word 'authentic' in 'eco authentic' is important because every supplier is promoting their eco credentials but some really invest their whole business ethos in the principle. A research study by Getty Images of 10,000 people globally reports that 81% of consumers see themselves as being eco friendly whilst only 50% buy from brands that try to be eco-friendly; this may on the face of it seem like a hypocritical statistic, they like the idea but when it comes to price or convenience, ecology suddenly loses its' importance, but it's still a very healthy 50% of the world looking for eco friendly products.

Group or collective buying.

This process offers products or services at reduced prices to a group of a minimum number of buyers. Group buying is most usually promoted online and fulfilled instore, when enough buyers commit to purchase the seller authorises the sale at the discounted price and the consumers each receive a voucher to be honoured in a retail outlet. This system is strong in India and China and popular with small retailers as a means of generating increased sales. Another more informal version is where shoppers join together and approach a seller to negotiate a group discount for the volume that they are able to offer, this idea is most commonly used for consumer durables, i.e. higher priced items.

Livestream shopping

This medium fuses traditional online ecommerce of the QVC type with entertainment, live video, content marketing, or with influencers broadcasting live on streaming platforms showcasing products, trying them on or presenting them and describing them to the viewer. Viewers can ask questions live and the offer flashes across the bottom of the screen. Now well established in China and about to explode in Europe and North America it is driven by a fun and creative experience; demonstrating how products work, new product launches, backstage access are some techniques. Consumers report that they find livestream shopping to be more social and interactive. The size of the livestream market in China is approaching $20bn.

There are two things that matter for this medium, the first is that the presentation must really be entertaining and the second having an influencer who is able to genuinely inspire trust in the audience. If the audience knows for example, that the influencer has tested the product on a sincerely independent basis then this will remove a lot of the barriers to purchase.

Consumers like the medium because without photoshopping or video editing they can be sure that what they are seeing is authentic, they can interact with the presenter live, it's a two way conversation. It is as close to visiting a store as is possible, online.

The medium is open to a wide range of businesses from farmed goods to luxury products, shoppers can choose their area of interest and tune in to small niche areas. It is a 'nowhere to hide' format, once live, it remains live until the end and so professional livestreamers spend a lot of time preparing for a broadcast before going live.

Augmented and virtual reality (AR/VR)

The ability for consumers to try products in their own homes, or in-store. Virtual reality replaces what you see, augmented reality adds digital elements to a live view. The IKEA Place app' is a good example of AR technology being used for a commercial purpose, it allows customers to see the furniture in their own environment.

There are plenty of other examples too, clothing retailer ASOS uses AR to create their Virtual Catwalk, the user clicks the 'AR' button on the appropriate page and then models appear giving a different view of the product. Manchester City, a UK football club, uses AR to allow fans to 'visit' the stadium and sit next to the club manager.

Gucci uses AR to allow you to 'try' on their shoes, the user points their camera at their feet to see a visual representation of how a particular shoe will look on their feet. Colour manufacturer Dulux uses AR to allow you to see what your room might look like when painted in a different colour. The user uses their own smartphone to detect the wall edges and then dictates the area to be coloured. Cosmetics retail Sephora has a 'Virtual Artist' to allow consumers to see what their products will look like when applied, lipstick or eyeshadow for example. There are many examples and the breadth of application is seemingly infinite.

From a practical viewpoint, you can use augmented reality with a smartphone, virtual reality requires special equipment.

Omni channel and unified commerce Omni channel commerce means having contact points with customers across several channels, best demonstrated with an example, imagine that a customer visits your website looking for a product but doesn't purchase there and then, browsing Facebook they see your ad', click through and are presented with an offer, after purchase they choose to pick up the product in-store; the customer has interacted with you in three different places. Consumers move between devices and channels, estimates vary between 70 and 90%, but in either case it's the large majority. Probably the worlds' biggest example is Amazon, accessible on laptop, tablet, mobile, smartwatches, Alexa, you can see the same account and order information whichever the device.

Unified commerce allows a retailer to manage all their sales systems from one backend system. Unified commerce takes the omni channel the experience and merges all the backend systems to support it, order fulfilment, inventory, customer relationship management, sales data etc to supply consistent data, in effect breaking down the walls between the various systems to deliver a common commerce platform. There are many advantages of a unified commerce system but the one of most interest here is that it supports customers in being able to start, stop, continue and finish shopping when and however they wish with consistent data. Today this is the accepted standard, not some wild aspiration.

But let's get back to why all this is important for the consumer. Here is an example of why it helps you to get this right. This story concerns a large UK supermarket, we needn't embarrass them by naming them. Ligia loves to try anything new, she saw a pack of Pigs in Blankets tea bags, they tasted as bad as you might imagine, in our view, a terrible product idea, she Tweeted this view in light hearted fashion and immediately received an apology plus a voucher to cover the cost and no need to return the product. More recently she bought a blouse from the same store and on trying it on at home noticed a hole in the sleeve, returning it to the store to ask for a replacement she was met with strong resistance, in fact she gave up and tried again, this time asking for the Manager to be summoned before she got the replacement. Firstly this is a clear example of commerce that is not unified, the business shows two very different faces and one can speculate that a Tweet is public, and a face to face interaction is not and so the store can afford to stand their ground as the chances are that no one other than the customer will hear about it. So what are we to make of this, on the one hand a business who gives a generous, indeed overly generous response as Ligia was only commenting about the teabags, not demanding a refund and on the other hand getting to a stand off where she was accused of returning goods that she had damaged. As a consumer what do you tell your friends? Is this a business that you trust and deals fairly with its' customers, or the reverse?

Artificial intelligence, chatbots and social media apps

Let's start with Artificial Intelligence and an example. Microsoft and Uber use Knightscope K5 robots to patrol parking lots and large outdoor areas and to predict and prevent crime. The robots can read license plates, report suspicious activity, and collect data to report to their owners. You can rent these R2-D2-like robots for $7 an hour and they don't need, holidays, pensions or time off sick.

According to Techgrabyte 'Artificial intelligence is the biggest commercial opportunity for companies, industries, and nations over the next few decades' and 'will increase global GDP by up to 14% between now and 2030,' which means that 'Latecomers will find themselves at a serious competitive disadvantage within the next several years'.

AI can analyse consumer behaviour and search patterns, and use data from social media platforms and blog posts to help businesses understand how customers find their products and services.

Artificial Intelligence will soon be the driving force behind many services and, currently, we already see it implemented in such areas as:

- Basic communication
- Product recommendations
- Content creation
- Email personalisation
- E-commerce transactions

One exciting example of AI in practice is chatbots, in case they're a new concept to you here is a definition, a computer program designed to simulate conversation with human users. This AI-based technology uses instant messaging to chat in real-time, day or night, with your customers or site visitors. Mastercard created a Facebook Messenger bot which uses natural language processing software to decipher what the customer wants and respond as if it were a real person – to automate payment handling. Chatbots 'learn' with experience and many consumers are unaware that they are communicating with a computer, and whether they do or not, chatbots are popular.

- Chatbots already power about 85% of customer service contact. Source: Innovation Enterprise.
- Chatbots give 24-hour service, instant responses to inquiries and simple questions.

It is estimated that within the next two years chatbots will help businesses save over $8 billion per annum. Source: Impactbnd.

Many customers prefer interacting with chatbots as they are responsive 24/7, give answers promptly, accurately recall your entire buying history, and never lose patience. They offer outstanding customer service by meeting customers' expectations and automating repetitive tasks.

The reality of modern marketing is that it is conversational, people want immediate answers, they now expect it to be that way. The standard now is no longer 'we'll get back to you', it's immediate, if your business cannot operate this dynamically you are now uncompetitive.

Natural language processing is what it is all about, computers are ideal for rule following formats such as spreadsheets but consider colloquial vocabulary, accents, different languages, humour, inference and nuance in human communication, a challenge for computers. But it's clear that great advances have been made and will continue, we are all familiar with voice recognition, it has its' occasional frustrations but it is good enough to have moved into our homes already. Affective computing is something that worries some of us, the ability of computers to understand and replicate human emotion. Technology has moved towards the analysis of unstructured rather than structured data, think about analysing Twitter, billions of lines of text and the challenge is to extract the value from that as it applies to your product or service. This is key to listening to what your customers think about you but, with, as we have seen billions of messages, way beyond the capability of human intervention.

You will no doubt have heard the term 'Big data', referring to the enormous data sets that are now routinely collected, volumes of data that were unthinkable not long ago. Data are valuable, in fact we heard this quote on the radio recently, 'datum is the new oil'. Just consider for a moment how much data most of us routinely give away, our age, address, relationship status, income, friends and contacts, where we holiday, every journey we ever make, who we speak to, what we buy and this is not a complete list, all these data are analysed computationally to reveal patterns, trends, and associations. You can see the result of this most evidently when you enquire about a product or service and then get bombarded with ad's. Why do we give this all away? In return for the 'free' use of social media. Is it a fair exchange? The reason for introducing this here is to focus on the commercial value of data and the reason why your business should engage with the process. Most businesses will post on social media and assume that the process has been completed, it will not have been.

If you wish to stand out you need to personalise your marketing which means personalised content, products, emails and more.

Consider these statistics:

- 63% of consumers are highly annoyed with generic advertising blasts.
- 80% say they are more likely to do business with a company if it offers personalised experiences. Source: Epsilon.
- 90% claim they find personalisation appealing. Source: Epsilon.

'Personalised, triggered emails based on behaviour are 3x better than batch-and-blast emails'. *Source: EmailMonks*. These figures are not really surprising are they but sometimes we need to see the numbers to really absorb what we inherently know.

Video marketing is one of, if not the, most important marketing trend today and likely to be so for the next 5-10 years. Here are some statistics that show the importance of incorporating video into your digital marketing strategy:

- 70% of consumers say that they have shared a brand's video.
- 72% of businesses say that video has improved their conversion rate.
- 52% of consumers say that watching product videos makes them more confident in online purchase decisions.
- 65% of consumers visit the marketer's website and 39% call a vendor after viewing a video.

Social Messaging Apps

POWERFUL BUSINESS RULES, EXTRAORDINARY RESULTS

The volumes of activity on social messaging app's are simply mind boggling, see some of these numbers:

1.3 billion users are active on Facebook Messenger every month.

10 Billion messages are sent between people and businesses on Facebook Messenger every month

WhatsApp has 1.6 billion active users and 55 billion messages are sent every day.

The top three social messaging apps, WhatsApp, Facebook Messenger and WeChat have more combined users than Facebook or YouTube.

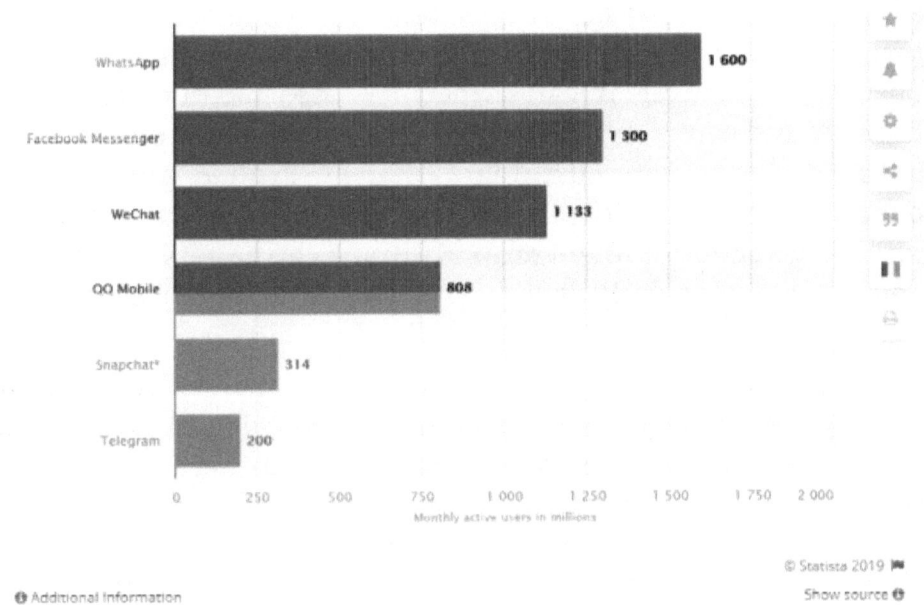

These statistics show the popularity of social messaging app's, and since people are spending more time messaging each other, it makes sense to market your company's products and services where your potential customers are hanging out.

Social messaging app's can be very useful in sending messages to customers directly, as they allow for personalisation and add value to the user experience. In addition, people expect businesses to have a presence on messaging app's because it's a direct and easy way to interact with them.

Sentiment analysis

We briefly mentioned analysis of unstructured data, but let's explore this topic further. You may have heard of sentiment analysis already but we will start from the beginning here as it may be new to you. Whichever it is, if you use social media you have been and are the subject of sentiment analysis. We will explain here what it is and why it is relevant to your business. Briefly put, sentiment analysis is text analysis and classification to determine whether the sentiment behind the comment is negative, positive or neutral, it can sometimes also include somewhat positive and somewhat negative. The text referred to here is the online chat that your customers engage in around your product or service, the analysis is an automated procedure. The volume of on-line chat and comment around a brand can be very substantial and so sentiment analysis is a tool for aggregating and summarising all these data to come to a useful conclusion.

If you use social media you have agreed to a trade off, as we have already discussed, you get access free of charge but in return the social media companies harvest and sell your data. Some companies are now buying social media data to link to their customer relationship management systems, so they can know a lot more about you than whatever you offer over the 'phone or by email.

Does this all matter? Well that depends on your viewpoint but the current debate is between government agencies who want data to be unencrypted and accessible, for security reasons, and the data companies who prefer to encrypt and thus have no access. The point of bringing this to your attention is that it demonstrates where technology is taking marketing and customer relations which can hopefully help direct your thinking about your own systems.

The tool used by data miners to find these opinions is called NLP (natural language processing). An NLP system is built to extract opinions from text and to be able to determine the difference between words automatically, simple phrases such as 'I like this product', or being able to classify the clear difference between 'this product is great' and 'this product in not great' also being aware of the emphasis in 'I really like this product'.

We have heard sentiment analysis described as like having a private detective listening to what your customers are saying, everywhere, indeed there is no other way of harvesting the information from the vast range of comment and interaction across all platforms. Your customer service and sales teams will pick up feedback of course but the 100% honest view will be available online. Whether it be good or bad feedback you know very well that these mediums of exchange will be closest to the truth.

It will come as no surprise to understand that there is considerable expertise and programming skill behind sentiment analysis systems, so not a field for the gifted amateur, but there are a growing number of suppliers who will be eager to work with you if you wish to pursue this.

Here are a few practical examples of where sentiment analysis fits in:

Brand mentions. If you own a brand then you need to track every time your brand is mentioned and in what context.

Mitigating bad customer experiences. No one gets it right all the time, the way that information can be spread these days if a motivated customer can be bothered to spend the time, and some surely will, one bad experience can come back to bite you many times over. If something has been picked up in the market then it helps your customer service team to know what is coming and to be prepared with a solution.

Find brand influencers. These people are important to you, consumers listen to them because they are seen to be impartial.

What are they saying about you? Do you need to react?

Product analysis. What do your customers love and hate about your product or service? If enough people are shouting then you have the opportunity to react and perhaps gain a competitive advantage.

Market research. If you are launching something new then getting an early response from the market will allow you to modify and adjust your offer as you proceed and perhaps before too much has been invested.

Competition. What are your competitors doing better than you? Where are you taking the lead? This information can be fed back to your product development and marketing operations.

9. GETTING NEW BUSINESS

This section gives some tips and ideas for developing new business as an established business, if you are a start-up then the ideas still have value, just read what is here with your own circumstances in mind.

Who is responsible for getting new business?

Perceived wisdom is that this is a sales function so, 'not my problem', in fact it is the responsibility of anyone who, visits, services, talks to, emails or writes to a client or potential client. The reason is that every touch point with a client influences the commercial relationship for better or sometimes worse and is also an opportunity to find out what else the client may need and whether your business can satisfy that need.

Make this principle permeate through your organisation and make it the foundation on which all your employees work. The "it's not my problem, it's sales" is archaic within any organisation.

Where does new business come from?

New business comes from either current clients, selling them more of the same thing or new products or services or from finding new customers. Finding new business from existing customers is easier and cheaper. Easier because the clients knows you and (hopefully) like and trust you, if that were not true, they would move their business elsewhere. Cheaper because you can visit your clients and you understand their business already, you don't need to find them. Consider your business and answer the following:

- In nearly all cases every customer is a customer for other products and services, do you have what the customer wants to fulfil these additional needs?
- Does your customer base know everything that you offer?
- Do your customers think to recommend you?
- Do you ask your customers for more business and recommendations?
- You may be on top of all this already and have answered yes to all these questions but if you have, in our experience you will be very unusual, so please don't be too self-critical if you answered with more no's.

How do you present yourself and what you want to sell?

Are you better or worse than your competitors? We have touched on this point already but let's consider it again here. If you don't know the answer to this question then you need to find out, here are some ideas for doing that:

- Ask your customers, they will tell you.
- Make an enquiry via 'phone, email, website and judge the response, set your criteria first so that you can be objective and top of that list of criteria must be the speed of response.
- On line reviews and chatrooms.

We recently heard of a supplier who asked customers to complete a survey at the end of the purchase process, as soon as a negative response was given the survey was terminated. We can see their motivation, what better way to be able to say 100% of our respondents were completely satisfied customers, true enough but not very smart really. Customers are not fools, if their experience of your business is wildly at odds with your own 'customer backed' claims then it is hardly credible and most likely to be slated elsewhere on line. The most important aspect here though is that genuine, honest and justifiable complaints are pure gold, they tell you exactly what you need to do to improve your business and probably how to do it too.

Have you ever had a great initial meeting, delivered your killer proposal, then heard nothing? Did you follow up? No, we didn't always do that either. If you listened carefully when you met your prospect and took the time to understand what was needed, fished a little to find out possible objections and the decision-making process and still didn't get the sale then what happened? Very often it can be something really minor, something that is easily within your power to resolve but your potential customer does not know that, this is why you invite objections.

Objections are your best friend.

Here's a thought, maybe your price was the problem, perhaps you cannot move on the price but you can offer better terms, split payments, a discount for early settlement, there may be many solutions to what could actually be a minor hitch. But if you don't invite objections you may never have that opportunity.

Can you explain your business in 15 seconds?

Can you describe your business to someone you have just met, exactly what you do and why are you different, in one sentence and without confusing or boring them? If not, sit down and write it out, try it out on someone who knows nothing about what you do, ask them to repeat your line back to them, did they get it?

Think about how you feel when you meet someone, you will ask what they do because it's polite and it opens the conversation, but are you really interested in the answer? If you get a quick succinct resumé you will understand what you have been told and if it touches your world somehow then you are likely to develop the conversation, if not then you switch off. I started a new service business a few years ago and attending a conference, I sought out the main influencer in the room, here was my big chance to sell my business idea, I was unprepared, I waffled, her eyes were soon scanning the room for an escape route, a wasted opportunity but a lesson learnt.

Do you impress your clients?

Do you exceed clients' expectations EVERY time? If not then how can you do that? This matters because you want to keep your customers, get more business from them and get them to recommend you. This point sits well with the section on over delivery, if it's not fresh in your mind perhaps revisit it to reinforce this point. Getting your existing customers to fall deeper in love with you is much easier than having to romance new ones.

If you are not better than or the same as your competitors then what can you offer to make your offer special? Here are some ideas that may help:

- Free information via webinars, emails or seminars, give them information that they need and want, not necessarily the same thing as what you want to tell them!
- A quarterly business review, this works well for service industries or where contracts or projects apply. Your customer will most likely have a clear idea of where they are with you but the point of this is to ask them about their problems to find out if there is anything else you can help them with. Also to deepen your relationship with them and to 'wave the flag' for your business.
- An invitation to visit the offices, play golf, have dinner…

whatever Some people feel comfortable with this sort of approach, others not, if any of this feels natural to you then make the offer.

- If you are providing a service then a monthly phone call, how are things going? Did you resolve ...... from when we last spoke? If it's a large product sale then a follow up call, your instinct is probably to put the money in the bank and move on but we are looking to be different, to over deliver, to delight, to be a talking point, to get referred.
- Or how about a small but personal gift? Small enough to not look like a bribe, a 'thanks for the order', 'thanks for thinking of us'.

New clients

Where does new business come from? Emails, calls, referrals? Is every enquiry handled quickly, politely and efficiently? When an enquiry is handled do you get some personal information and start to create a relationship? Do you ask questions about their business to understand how best to respond?

Consider that by the time someone has contacted you they have already probably passed through a good part of the purchasing cycle:

- They have identified their need.

- They have found a possible solution.

- They have found you and considered that you have what they need.

- They have looked at other suppliers and may be contacting them too.

- They have researched prices and may well already know what you will quote.

- They have looked at online reviews and possibly comparison sites.

This means that you may be halfway to a sale when the potential customer first makes contact with you. Therefore the questions posed in the first paragraph above become absolutely key, the potential customer is ready to talk, they are unlikely to be frustrated by your questions, they have made the first move and they want to hear more. The key to managing this process effectively is a systemised approach to ensure the quality of your response, it is easier to take the time to manage a 'ready to go' customer than find a new one yourself. Scripted marketing efforts are so tired these days as to be insulting but the trick is to manage the process without it seeming to have been over managed, some ideas:

- Find out how your competitors respond.
- Tell the customer that you have a list of questions, that sounds professional, but ask them personally, don't obviously read from a list.
- Find out who in your organisation (or hire someone) who is comfortable answering calls and emails in a personable way, chatty without talking too much, interested without being intrusive, and direct enquiries to that person.
- LISTEN to what they have to say, and do not under any circumstance ignore a direct question.
- Try and be different. This needs thought and application to your product or service but something extra, something that they weren't expecting.

When you respond do you ask for the business? Some people hate directness but this is business after all, are you buying or not? If not is there anything that I can do to make this work for you? It comes back to our comments about objections, very often a block to a sale is something that you are able to easily resolve if you find out what it is.

What can you do to make every new enquirer think your business is personally engaged with them and that their business matters to you? Let's face it, the number one name at the top of everyone's agenda is their own, how can you make every customer, new or old, feel valued? How can you make sure that this happens every time, all the time?

Why should potential clients choose you? you need to have a clear, simple and convincing answer to this. Avoid competitor bashing, it sounds, and is, weak.

Ask everyone in your business to come up with three ideas and five things that they plan to do to get more business. There is always a huge amount of enthusiasm, knowledge, experience and creativity in any organisation and usually buried under a deep pile of resentment, why? Because everyone sees a little bit of the overall picture and has a different view, not even the best CEO has eyes and ears everywhere, and the norm' is that people are just not asked for their views or when they do eventually put their head above the parapet, they are ignored. Think laterally here, why wouldn't the old hand in accounts have a great marketing idea? And if you ask for ideas, act on them and be seen to act on them.

10. DEVELOPING EXPORT MARKETS

Once you have established your business close to home, exporting can seem like a cheap and easy way to grow sales exponentially and without the same investment that it took to get your business to where it is already. If you are new to exporting let us start by making two points, firstly exporting is a skill in its' own right and secondly don't make the mistake of treating it lightly. Let us expand on this second point a bit, it's a common misconception that you can dump product in an export market, put the cheque in the bank and enjoy the profits, this is a mistake because to maximise the potential of any market you need to develop it with the same care and attention that you would with the home market otherwise your experience will be short lived.

How to start and ensure that you succeed

New markets can be very expensive and failures more costly than at home, why:

- The time and cost of travel
- The time it takes to understand the trading environment
- The cost of ensuring your goods meet local regulations

- Market testing
- And, simple mistakes are easy to make and can cost a lot

Here's a simple mistake that cost a lot. A gentleman that we met, the owner of a manufacturing company making shampoo for pets in the UK found a distributor in Mexico, he shipped his stock to a warehouse in the US and then onto his new distributor and then to retailers throughout the country. He never received a second order. He had no one in the business who spoke Spanish and the distributor was similarly linguistically limited. The problem turned out to be that compliance with Mexican standards required an adjustment to the labelling to include some additional wording, in Spanish, not a big deal in itself but in this case it resulted in the withdrawal of the product from the market and the end of the trading relationship.

Which markets?

The answer to this point is determined by a few variables:

1. Practical considerations, does anyone on the team have experience or knowledge of a market? Language skills that could be useful? Do you already have contacts or trusted partners anywhere?
2. Look at the non-tariff barriers, free trade agreements and labelling and health and safety regulations. All countries protect their citizens by imposing safety standards but those regulations are different and have different licensing procedures, Europe for example, imposes a different version of safety standard than the US, sometimes this can be an adjustment to labelling, but it can involve time consuming and costly testing. The point here is that you may wish to consider the easier route to market if you are new to exporting.
3. Are any markets culturally or otherwise aligned with yours? This could make your product easier to launch.

Expat' communities can sometimes be a good starting point for introducing your offer to an overseas market.

Research

Be honest with yourself, realistic and open minded, ask the questions and challenge the answers. Being realistic at the beginning will save you time and money.

- Why will the market or service want my product? New? Different? Cheaper? If you don't know then you need to find out.
- Can I sell competitively in the market?
- Why will a distributor be interested to take your product? Good margin? Promotional support? Fits their business?

The same rules apply as in your domestic market so there is no need to repeat the detail but given geographic, linguistic and cultural differences you should consider finding an advisor. The cost of an advisor is likely to be a lot less that the cost of visiting and spending time in a market yourself, flights, hotels, time away from the business..... and the results more accurate.

Market testing

Once you have answered the basic questions the next step is testing your product or service:

- Testing allows you to make your mistakes cheaply
- Shipping stock to the market is hugely expensive
- A distributor will only be disappointed once
- Very often minor issues can destroy a project, testing gives you the opportunity to adjust your offer

How do you market test: If you have a good relationship with a partner in the market they can present your product or service and give you the feedback.

If you have found a distributor, they may be willing to work with you.

Either way, the acid test is to put your product or service in front of a buyer and ask them to pay for it – and listen to the response.

The two key points to settle are, is there a demand and can you sell for a profit? We know that that sounds devastatingly simplistic but amidst the heady excitement of new contacts, countries and markets, the basics often get lost.

How do I find a trading partner?

Most exporters will seek a distributor or partner, it saves time, money and by working hand in hand can avoid many of the simple mistakes that can easily be made when entering a new market.

You may have contacts already, you may find introductions through trade bodies or you may need to start from scratch.

In whichever case, you have one chance to impress.

Is your offer competitive in the market? Do you know why your potential partner will want to trade with you? What's in it for them? Are they offering competitor products or services? What marketing support are you prepared to give? What training can you offer?

When you start a trading relationship it is a negotiation and this is what your new partner will be looking for:

- ✓ A product or service that complements his or her current offer, something that makes his business more interesting to his or her customers
- ✓ A good margin
- ✓ A product or service that his or her customers want, this may sound very obvious but I can assure you that this point is often forgotten or ignored
- ✓ Confidence in you as a supplier

- ✓ Support, a sense of partnership
- ✓ Continuity of quality and supply

And this is what you need:
- ✓ A partner for whom your product or service has the potential to add enough to their business to make them really work hard to sell it
- ✓ A reliable payer
- ✓ Market contacts that can establish your product or service quickly and easily so, credibility and a good reputation in the market.

The closer you get to fulfilling each other's needs the sooner you will have an agreement; start trading and the more chance you will have of a successful long-term relationship – a bit like dating when you think about it!

For you, the way to get the best deal is to be prepared by which we mean that the better you have undertaken your research and the more knowledge you have, the stronger your negotiating position and the more convincing your proposal. At the initial stages, establishing credibility on both sides is the first hurdle.

So here are a few tips that we hope may be helpful:

- Try and find a partner of similar size, it's tempting to think that biggest is best but we disagree with that logic for three reasons, it's an uneven negotiation if the proposed partner is bigger, your product or service is much less likely to impact their world, and it needs to, and thirdly because we have witnessed this process many times and have rarely seen the small supplier/big distributor agreement work well or for very long.
- Allow your partner to make good money out of the deal, don't screw them down for every last cent, this is because if they make a good living out of selling your prod-

uct or service they will work harder for you, your name will open every conversation that they have with their clients, not be left until last or even forgotten. If you have done your research you should already know what margins your new partner is likely to expect before you meet face to face.

- Be honest at all times, in particular with regard to deliveries, reorders etc, if it will take you one week to deliver tell them two and give them a nice surprise – remember our new friend over delivery?

- Think the whole process through from order to delivery and make sure you have everything covered, discussed and understood. The lure of a new customer brings exciting thoughts of big profits to mind, lower overheads as your manufacturing volumes increase and the excitement of seeing what has probably been your baby, in other parts of the world, but don't lose sight of what matters now. What matters at this point is the detail and most importantly making sure it all runs without a hitch, you have an opportunity to impress your client. Make sure that the payment terms are fair and give you enough cash flow to manage the business, that you have a comfort margin in your delivery schedule, that your packing and transportation procedures are in place, that you have properly understood and addressed any labelling and health and safety issues. In other words the deal is the excitement, the boring detail is what can trip you up.

- To make things work you and your partner need to align systems, no effort is wasted to get this right, you already have the business. Once systems are aligned then subsequent orders should flow easily. Here are some problems that we have witnessed which have stopped the order flow and added time to the supply and delivery process. Documentation inside the delivery carton so not visible on the outside, wrong sized pallet which doesn't match the distributors storage system, invoices with insufficient information to pass clearance for payment, hazardous goods not separated, outer carton size containing more or less units than specified, distributor system not updated with all the required information to recognise a product..... the list goes on but the point of drawing your attention to this is to demonstrate how missing small details can generate huge problems.

So with this last point in mind don't be afraid to suggest a small trial order to stress test the systems. We would argue that your new partner is most likely to be impressed by your care and attention if you take the time to explain the issue.

Is my trading partner financially secure?

However you meet it is simple due diligence to check the financial standing of your potential partner and whether they can and do pay their bills on time. Credit agencies can provide this information for you. No business is worth having unless you get paid, and paid on time. At its' worst a small supplier delivering a huge order and not receiving payment can, and does, bankrupt small suppliers, you are very likely to have your own anecdotes, it's such a common story. If it helps add a sense of urgency, think of it like this, you are giving your assets, your cash to a third party, you need to be really sure that your assets are safe.

How can I protect my interests before shipping stock?

Any agreement will necessarily be managed by a contract under the legislation of the country of origin or destination and this will of course govern the responsibilities of both parties, payment terms, marketing support and when the ownership of the stock passes.

The usual process will be for your partner to present you with an agreement for signature, it is unusual, perhaps unheard of, for you to be presented with a document that favours your interests. The contract will have been written, or at least edited, by a lawyer acting for your partner and these documents can be mind blowingly complex and over worded and sometimes in a language unfamiliar to you. Legal advice is of course essential but the point to consider here is that you are still negotiating, you have both decided that you like each other and want to work together so that's no longer the issue, it's tweaking the last little bit of advantage and each trying to give themselves the maximum room to manoeuvre. So a lot of words here but the practical point is never sign anything you cannot live with but be fair and recognise that you can't have it all your own way either.

Mexican legal work is one of the specialities of our Consultancy and we acted for an artist who had been approached by a publisher in Mexico who wanted to print and distribute her work, the value of the contract was considerable but the document in Spanish and she is English. The temptation for her was to be excited by the big numbers and sign, well it was money she hadn't been expecting, but she gave it to us for an opinion and we were very quickly able to negotiate the very one sided document back to something that we could advise our client to sign and also check for her, the bona fides of her new partner. The point of relating this anecdote is to make the point that whilst a partner may present a contract that favours themselves, sometimes outrageously so, they do ultimately understand that the document has to be fair for both sides and so pushing back a bit at this stage to get what is fair is not going to lose the business.

If you prefer a less confrontational approach then agreeing the key points that both parties wish to be included, known as 'Heads of Terms', allows both parties to outline what is fair to be included and what is expected in the agreement so that when a full contract is presented there should be no big surprises and subsequent discussion will just be around the detail. Here are the

key points that should be contained in any agreement: The main terms: -   The parties involved.
- Product or service range.
- Brand and trade marks and names.
- Territory.
- Length of agreement.
- Specific obligations of both parties.
- Payment terms.
- Sales forecasts.
- Right of renewal (protection for the distributor) if forecasts achieved.
- Confidentiality.
- Termination.
- Jurisdiction in case of controversy

Where do you start?

Time and investment are needed but the advice is to take small inexpensive steps and invest more as your confidence in the viability of your product or service as a profitable exercise in your target market grows.

Undertake your due diligence and make objective decisions at each stage.

So to quickly reiterate, you need to find the answers to the following questions:

<u>Is there a market for my product or service in my chosen export market?</u>

You love your product or service so objectivity may be difficult but it is the key, undertake the research phase carefully and completely and if you find it difficult to detach yourself to analyse the results, get someone else to do it and to give you a fair unbiased summary.

Can I sell my product or service in my chosen export market and make a profit?

The chapter on costing and pricing takes you through this process if it is new to you, for export markets there are additional things to consider such as international transportation, customs clearance and duties and the effect of different currency if you are selling in the local currency, but the process is just the same. Top down from market prices, bottom up from your cost base and hopefully a nice big gap in the middle which is your margin.

It is foolish to spend time and money visiting a market if you have not properly completed a thorough viability assessment, why? Because this can be undertaken quite cheaply and identify any major blockages before too much has been invested, or allow you the opportunity to adjust your offer.

We have previously discussed the importance of protecting any brand, trading names, patents or intellectual property that you own so we don't need to revisit here. However if you intend to exploit any of these in an overseas market then we would add a further point which is that if a distributor or other trading partner helps you to develop business in their market, then whatever may subsequently happen to your trading relationship with them, good or bad, you will continue to own the business, not them!

Here we have created a fictitious brand 'Mexcafé' to show the processes, the analysis work is however, factual and applies to the UK market. Here are some extracts from the study to demonstrate the process.

The information was accurate at the date the research was undertaken.

Coffee is an important product in Mexico and a growing market in the UK so we considered how a Mexican grower could approach the UK market.

Company registration

The first step would be to check that the name 'Mexcafé' is not already registered, it may be that you would not want a company structure at this early stage but it is still important to know if the name is available and consideration given to registering the name immediately to secure it and leaving the company dormant; this requires a small amount of paperwork but no operating cost.

In the case of our example, Mexcafé Limited is available.

Trademark registration

Trademark registration is essential at the start of investment in an export market, without securing this the danger is to develop a valuable market and later find that someone else owns your valuable asset or that they stop you using it.

In the case of our example, here's what we found: The 'Mexcafé' trademark available but interestingly a similar brand name Mexicafé has already been registered in the following classes:

25 Clothing footwear headgear

29 Foodstuffs - meat fish, fruit, vegetables, eggs and dairy products

30 Foodstuffs – Coffee, tea, flour, bread, sugar and confectionery

33 Alcoholic drinks (except beers)

43 Restaurant and accommodation services

So we can see that a similar brand is registered in the UK and so we would now focus our investigation on looking to see where and how the similar brand is being used. From a practical viewpoint it makes little sense to enter a market with a brand or trademark that is likely to be confused with one that is already in use and particularly if there is a prospect of potential legal action. In our example we were unable to find the brand name being used.

If a name that you wish to use is already registered you have two options, firstly if the name has been registered but you cannot find it being used you may wish to contact the owner and ask if he or she wishes to sell their rights to you, the second option is to start with a new brand. Whilst this can be expensive, new packaging and publicity materials etc it is a well trodden path, many global brands appear under different guises in different markets. The US fast food chain KFC appears as PFK (Poulet Frit Kentucky) in French speaking Quebec. American Lays crisps became Walkers in the UK when Lay's owner bought Walkers, to retain the brand following that it enjoyed in the UK. And closer to our example above, the Unilever brand Axe was originally launched in France but when it was exported it was discovered that the brand was already registered in many markets and so the range was rebranded as Lynx.

Domain name registration

The next step is to secure your online presence, so for our example brand, Mexcafé we discovered that all these domain names are available:

www.mexcafe.co.uk/.net/.org/.club/.info/.uk

www.mexcafes.com

www.mexcafe.cafe

www.mexacepro.com/.club

www.mexcafe.online

www.mexcafeonline.club

www.mexcafe.eu

www.themexcafe.com

You may choose to secure anything close to your area of interest as well as the site that you will want to use. The processes shown here are the basic procedures that we would undertake for a new business, there is of course very much more to it but this will secure a presence and most importantly, the investment in the market. We wanted a first hand view from someone who had successfully entered an export market.

We spoke to Katya Torres de la Rocha Managing Director of Mexgrocer a UK supplier of specialist Mexican food products in the UK, Mexgrocer is well established in the UK market and we were interested to hear about the journey, here's what Katya Torres de la Rocha had to tell us.

> 'Mexgrocer started in 2006 but I bought it in 2009, I was a restaurateur before in Mexico City, the UK and Madrid so I had already established commercial relationships with other importers in Europe and producers in Mexico. I noticed how difficult was to find authentic Mexican ingredients, I also saw the increase in e-commerce so I just connected the dots. In 2006 Mexican food was named by UNESCO as an inheritance of the world and at the same time Mexican food started to grow in popularity.
>
> The UK market is very open minded about other cuisines and people are very willing to try, Mexican food is little known, but that has been the opportunity for my business. There is a lot of red tape and legislation when it comes to food and alcohol in the UK, it has been a long journey of learning. British people are very positive about Mexico and Mexican products, anyone from the UK who has visited Mexico speaks about how wonderful the country and the food is.
>
> Getting MexGrocer known in the UK was my first challenge, I used every means, recommendation from clients, social media, newspapers, magazines, but mainly through people looking for us when they need ingredients. I have found the UK to be a very open market for Mexican products but success here requires a professional and measured approach'.

11. FINANCING YOUR BUSINESS

How much and where does it come from? Let's start with two questions, how much can you afford to lose if your big idea doesn't work out? And can you think of any reason why anyone would want to take the same risk as you, on your idea?

The first question is not a challenge, it may be nothing or it may be a lot, either can be managed, the point is to be clear that if you are going to risk personal capital then make sure that you decide at the beginning what you can lose and still sleep at night, and never deviate; don't be like the loser at the casino accumulating losses chasing the next big win. Make your decision up front and be sure to make the consequences clear to and get the willing agreement of whoever else may be affected.

The second question is to focus on how lenders think. Banks present themselves as being warm and fluffy and many people consider them to be the devil, but the truth is that they are businessmen who look at risk and reward. If you offer a safe and good return on investment they will be with you, and as soon as that landscape changes they will be gone. If you are not prepared to risk your assets they will wonder why they should risk theirs either, unless you are prepared to give guarantees (such as the equity in your house), they are not in the business of taking gambles or getting over excited about your big idea.

If you and whoever else would be affected by loss of personal capital are in agreement and you all face and accept the worst case, before you start, then if things become rougher than you hoped then you will not face the additional agony of a personal crisis too.

- So these are the options when it comes to finance.
- You fund from savings or better still ,revenues.
- You use personal assets to guarantee funds (usually the equity in your house).
- You use the assets in the business to guarantee funds.
- You trade equity for investment.
- You piggy back with someone else.

The first option is in our view the golden ticket but you may be less risk averse than us, there is a system for doing this which we explain below.

Clearly separate your personal and business assets right from the begining and protect the former. Some people persuade themselves down the route of thinking that if they don't take the risk then they don't really believe in the idea. We don't go along with this, we take the view that personal and business finance should always be separated, if you want to sell a personal asset and put the proceeds into your business then at least your personal assets remain protected. The structure of the business that you intend to operate should also be considered at this point, whether you are acting as an individual or under the protection of a company or corporation. This is a broader subject and the facts and options vary by country and so we will not pursue this here.

Business assets that a bank will look at are past profitable trading history, property owned by the business possibly including patents and intellectual property. If things don't work out banks will protect their own interests ruthlessly, if this sounds harsh remember that their first responsibility is towards their own shareholders.

Raising venture capital and what funders look for

The equity for investment route usually involves a venture capital company or sometimes a business incubator tied to a university business development unit. You sign over equity in return for cash, they are buying a part of your business in other words. Some of the most inequitable contracts that we have ever witnessed sit in this area. You might be thinking of the relief of seeing that wonderful lump of money sitting in your business account and be in a rush to sign anything, everything is negotiable and for this kind of relationship to work you really have to need each other in equal measure. VC companies will usually demand representation at board level and performance figures that won't leave you relaxing for a minute, they are only protecting their investment after all but they have a reputation for being very hard taskmasters. Don't dismiss the value of having an invested, interested, expert on your board either.

According to the article in the Harvard Business Review "How Venture Capitalists Really Assess a Pitch", Lakshmi Balachandra, Associate Professor at Babson College who undertook extensive research about the interaction between the VCs and Entrepeneurs 94% of VCs are male, therefore stereotypical gendered behaviours such as assertiveness and aggression may carry more weight than sensitivity and emotional awareness. This is not something that any of us probably wishes to read and whilst the situation is apparently slowly changing, one has to take a view with regard to the situation today.

Gianpiero Ptriglieri from INSEAD uses the word 'holding' to refer to the ability to hold the ship steady in rough seas, the ability to remain calm and make rational decisions when conditions are tough.

Agreements with third parties

Working with a third party can work very well if there is a strong complementarity between businesses, if for example you own a unique piece of technology that fits the offering of a company with the distribution that you need. This can also give your business a significant step up that may otherwise take you years to achieve. The options here are partnership or licensing agreements or joint venture agreements. We don't have the space to explore this here and it is veering off topic a bit so let's conclude this section by returning to basics.

How to start your business with little or no risk

Yes it can be done, it is slower than some of the financing routes presented above but it leaves you in complete control and without the pressures of financial worries.

This is where the internet becomes your very best friend because there is no market you cannot talk to through the internet and it is cheap to do so. If the internet has one overriding skill it is its' ability to find a niche, and cheaply.

So the approach is step by step and let's be clear, we are not talking about anything that requires large capital investment up front, but that aside with the ability to identify niche markets cheaply you can test and adjust your product offer, invest the profits in more stock and grow slowly but safely.

If you need to manufacture, get someone else to do it so you will have a product to test before you need to invest, your margins will be lower but so will your risk.

Test small batches on different platforms at different price points, you are unlikely to gain enough attention to establish your price in the market so your options will still be open.

So this is the slow growth option, testing gently, moving forwards using revenues earned and not borrowed and making sure that what you want to do next works, before taking the step. This will go against the rain for many because it's not the dynamic way forward and in truth the optimum is probably this plus some risk capital but if we leave you with one thought only, let it be this.

Think of your investment, time and capital, as investment chips, both are limited so you must make sure that you win more than you lose.

12. SOME FINAL THOUGHTS FROM THOSE THAT HAVE ALREADY DONE IT

Some advice from the worlds' self-made billionaires. The list below includes people who between them have been responsible for creating hundreds of billions of dollars of wealth, so what can they tell you? Well no one has the whole picture but each offers a different perspective so please extract from this whatever inspires you.

Bill Gates – Microsoft

Analyse any situation from every possible angle, then make a decision and stick with it. He emphasises the adverse effects of continually re-exploring decisions; he says it ends up "interfering not only with your execution but also with your motivation to make a decision." Thus, making a single decision, sticking with and seeing it through until the situation drastically changes is essential to avoid second-guessing yourself and interfering with your execution.

Jeff Bezos – Amazon

Bezos' critical piece of advice to anyone starting a business is to be a missionary (someone who loves and builds their customers and product or service) as opposed to a mercenary (someone who is obsessed with selling their company). In the long run, he believes that the missionary always beats out the mercenary in building a successful company. So, in short, make sure you love your customers and business and are prepared to build them up.

Warren Buffet – Berkshire Hathaway, investment

His advice for entrepreneurs is to simply have fun. He is famous for saying "at 85, I tap and dance to work every day". His main message here is enjoy what you do and have a passion for it, in his words, "there's nothing like it". For him, this is one of the key factors to being successful in any business.

Amancio Ortega – Zara, fashion retailer

'Speed is everything'. The ability to execute faster than your competitors and accelerate business processes is a hallmark of Ortega's success and something he recommends you adopt.

Mark Zuckerberg – Facebook

His advice for founders starting a new business is to try to solve a problem and be passionate about solving that problem. Don't try to build a company, that comes as a consequence of solving a problem.

Carlos Slim – Telecoms

His crucial management advice to new business owners is always to make sure you have "simple organisational structures" in place. Minimal hierarchies enable your business to act quickly and take advantage of opportunities that other companies cannot.

Larry Ellison – Oracle

One of Ellisons' most famous quotes is: 'great achievers are driven, not so much by the pursuit of success but by the fear of failure'. By this, he means you need to have the right mindset to achieve the success that some of the world's most exceptional entrepreneurs have, and you can do this not by just aiming for victory but by letting the fear of failure drive you beyond your limits.

Michael Bloomberg – Media

'If there's only one key to success, its hard work'. It is the simplest but perhaps the best piece of advice, since hard work and perseverance is what you will mainly need to build your business.

We really hope that reading this book has benefitted you as much we hoped, if you have any comments or questions we will be happy to hear from you and promise to respond, we can be contacted at 'jwright@lawbiz.co.uk'.

www.ingramcontent.com/pod-product-compliance
Lightning Source LLC
Chambersburg PA
CBHW031448210526
45464CB00005B/2366